THE CERTAINTY PRINCIPLE

$$C = \frac{H \cdot IN}{M \cdot Id \cdot O}$$

A formula for leadership
in uncertain times

David Douglass Light

The Certainty Principle
by David Douglass Light

Print Version
Published September 2020
ISBN: 978-1-7357799-0-4

L&S Ltd.
P.O. Box 77
West Point, PA 19454 USA

www.certain.im

Dedicated to David Martin

TABLE OF CONTENTS

INTRODUCTION

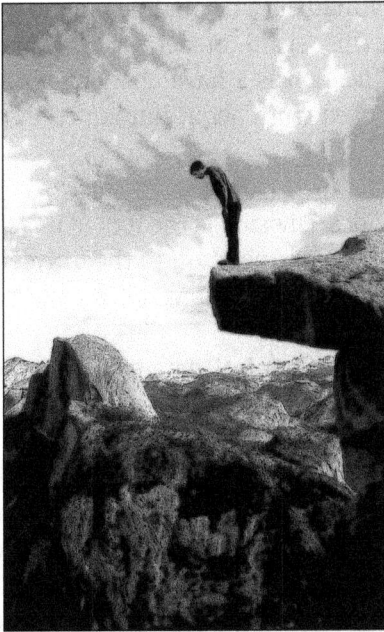

> "I was 100% certain I would not fall off,
> and that certainty is what kept me from falling off."
> ~ HONNOLD, 2015

DISCLAIMER:
I AM UNQUALIFIED AND
MY PRINCIPLES WON'T WORK FOR YOU.

Nothing I have written below will necessarily make you rich or beautiful, popular or famous. Nothing in my education or experience distinguishes or qualifies me to give any advice whatsoever in this regard. In fact, probably just the opposite. My only qualification is I have abandoned the fear of confronting the naked truth about human certainty, and how I can sustain it.

> The brain divides. Division is the root of uncertainty. There is nothing certain or uncertain in the universe except that the brain makes it so. Therefore, nothing is impossible.

The brain is a biochemical data-collecting device, evolved over eons for actioning (converting data into action) for survival. The brain digests data to extract decisions and actions just like the stomach digests and sorts nutrients for physical survival. At least that is how it should work. As we will see, the brain's primordial motive is binary decision-making, e.g., sustenance vs. starvation. The brain, through which nearly all data is processed, divides and decides. Modern human survival has evolved beyond mere physical survival to become dominated by identity survival. The brain tends to go to extremes to preserve and protect identity, even though, as we will see, identity is an illusion. This evolved state of division and decision is the source of all human uncertainty and suffering. Eliminating this mindset of uncertainty is its own reward.

CERTAINTY is the undivided equilibrium state. It is freedom from allowing uncertainty to dictate what I manifest in life. It is feeling comfortable being "at home in my own skin." Certainty is my anchor, set in my bedrock, embedded in my earth, spinning in my universe, unbounded by a limitless **HORIZON** in the time and scope limits of my brain's decisions and actions and incomes.

When I was a little kid there was no future. My horizon was mostly what I was going to do the next day. A couple of weeks to build and race my DIY go-cart down the hill behind our house was as good as my horizon got. Scope and time expanded a little as I grew older. But as it did, the confidence and resilient optimism that comes from a brain undivided succumbed to an attachment to vanity and outcome dependence. **THE CERTAINTY PRINCIPLE (TCP)** is about retraining my brain to be certain.

Certainty is the supremacy of control, independent of external conditions. Certainty focuses on my duty, the work of my authentic accountability while minimizing distractions. Cracking the code on a simple, workable formula for building and maintaining certainty is my challenge. There are methods available that seem complex and difficult, relying mainly on systems of faith and belief. These don't work for me. I want to understand the science of certainty, the mechanics based on fundamentals, based on knowledge rather than hope. I find this problem so interesting and important that I choose it as my duty (my mandate). As shown below, learning to limit my choices and actions to my **MANDATE** is a pillar of the TCP approach.

> *"As every divided kingdom falls,*
> *so every mind divided confounds and saps itself."*
> ~ DA VINCI, CA. 1520 (LDV)

If you, the reader, thinks the payoff of certainty is unclear or perhaps threatening, read no further. What follows will appear as sacrilegious to some as it is sublime for others — because, of the few assumptions that The Certainty Principle makes, one is that personal accountability for choice and action is absolute. As Pascal's story below illustrates, literally all I am is my choice of actions. Notice I say choice of action, not result. That's because outcomes of actions, to a greater or lesser degree, rely on a variety of independent influences beyond my control.

On December 6, 1941, my father was preparing to move to Puerto Rico to manage a sugar plantation and become an artist. The next day he was preparing for war.

> *"The best-laid schemes o' mice an' men*
> *Gang aft agley (often go wrong)."*
> ~ BURNS, KILMARNOCK EDITION, "TO A MOUSE," 1786

Outcomes are fundamentally unreliable, but my "Incomes" — my individual commitments to the outcome equation — are entirely reliable.

Reliance on outcomes, beyond the data they provide, diminishes certainty. My reliance on incomes (my production) increases certainty. Misery is the result of depending on outcomes. To avoid misery, I limit my exposure to outcome attachment while embracing my incomes, the net result of the application of my natural talents and skills. The outcomes of actions I'm poor at executing will always be poor. This is the remedy TCP provides. Reliance on outcomes is a reliable source of misery — fundamentally, fear and regret. Reliance on incomes is the reliable source of certainty, the harmony of optimism about those actions that are confidently within my control. It is easy to be optimistic when I learn to value the quality of my incomes as paramount.

My **INCOME** is the net production from my primary work on earth (my mandate). It must be measured and increased. Whatever measure(s) of achievement of my mandate I choose, my goal is growth. My metric can be quality, quantity, financial compensation, or all three. Mindful measurement creates certainty, even if I am seldom completely satisfied with the result.

> *"I have offended God and mankind because my work didn't*
> *reach the quality it should have."*
> ~ LdV — Melzi, 1519

That said, Leonardo didn't mind displaying the Mona Lisa for the public to see (He ended up loving the painting so much he never sold it.), despite its "imperfections." TCP tells us to try, try, and keep trying for excellence. The most important quality is the power of execution.

> *"A good plan violently executed now*
> *is better than a perfect plan executed next week."*
> ~ Gen. George Patton, 1947

There is always occasional distraction, but I do not waste time playing at things. Income, direction, and magnitude are the vectors of achievement. In their wake is the entire value of my time on earth — the performance of my mandate. I don't make honey and bees don't write books about Certainty. My mandated work creates value, as a honeybee's work creates honey. Likewise, the importance of my contribution is paramount, as viewed subjectively. Aspiration and competitiveness to achieve ever greater goals is only human. But assessment of my "personal best" through measurement, avoiding attachment to external comparisons, is the path to mastery. Certainty is knowing and mastering value-creation based on my individual mandate, absent any identification with either the mastery *per se*, or attachment to any particular outcome of the value created.

The honey bee (as far as I know) does not gloat over her honey work. Should her honeycomb be destroyed by storm, she begins rebuilding it because her mandate is building and repairing the hive. Reading the notes of Leonardo Di Vinci yields little self-reflective commentary. He focused his vast intellect on the perfect execution of his incomes.

Such focus on incomes may be for either virtuous or afflictive purposes. Mastering virtuous incomes serves value creation. Di Vinci's work, "Salvatore Mundi," stunned the art world with its uncanny beauty, (eventually) fetching nearly half a billion dollars in 2017. Mastering afflictive incomes serves value destruction. Adolph Hitler's mastery was at the root of a conflict resulting in nearly 75 million deaths.

TCP helps me distinguish between the two. Certainty elevates accountability to my incomes to the top, rationalizing everything else. My brain is that irascible data processing organ responsible for figuring out the difference. There are forces beyond my brain's meager capacity, or maybe anyone's, to understand. The brain has massive limitations. Just as there are physical limits on sensory data (seeing, hearing, etc.), there are processing limitations that are both intellectual (IQ) and systemic (the brain operates on a Boolean logic, [Boole, 1854]). What can be reasoned is limited because cognitive capacity is very finite. For example, "God" may help or hinder me, who knows? I relegate all such non-cognitive thoughts to chance and condition. Religion, magic crystals, aliens, or the Logos are beyond me. Therefore, conditional. I don't deny the existence of "reason-defying" influences. Quite the contrary. I know they exist, but TCP is a practical operating manual, not a philosophical work. TCP's purpose is to train the brain to cut a hard line between actionable priorities and the superfluous, particularly the latter. Programming my brain to excel at such choices is key to TCP — and to my subjective success.

At 10 I was free. Certainty came naturally. Concerns about who I was or what others thought of me disappeared with a chunk of Double-Bubble gum. Alternately, I played at being Davy Crockett or the drag-racer Don "Big Daddy" Garlits. When my buddies showed up on Saturdays to shoot targets or build a go-cart, I never gave a serious thought to myself. As I grew up, **IDENTITY** kicked in hard, and I became a slave to vanity. And that's when the trouble started. The first time I drove my cart down the "mountain" behind my house I crashed it into a bloody wreck. As I lay dazed, bleeding and broken looking up at my buddies, my first thought was not, "What an idiot! I obviously have no business building go-carts." Instead, it was, "God, I hope my Mother doesn't find out." That was followed quickly by, "I think it needs brakes."

OUTCOMES, e.g., go-cart wrecks, were not something I spent a lot of time fearing or regretting. They were data points, like the "needs brakes" response, signaling design improvements. Unfortunately, by age 14 the discovery of girls changed all that. Outcomes came to dominate my thinking and my emotions, often with crippling effect. Outcomes are only important for the data they provide.

When asked why he attempted to climb Mt. Everest, Sir James Mallory's (Mallory, 1923) famous, "Because it's there" represents manifest Certainty. To multitudes before him, attaining the summit of the world's highest mountain had no reality, or at most was a remote abstraction. To Mallory it was real enough to compel the actions required for getting there. That Mallory's Mt. Everest outcome was, ultimately, fatal does not diminish the importance of his three early attempts in the eyes of fellow mountaineers. In fact, it elevates him, particularly for the route-finding discoveries he made. One might say that Mallory (and partner Andrew Irvine) reached their own high peak of Certainty through their dogged commitment to climbing the then perilously unexplored mountain.

As with the discovery of Black Holes (both literally and figuratively) (Finkelstein, 1958), most interesting scientific studies result when there is a conspicuous lack of data discovery. Finkelstein began pursuing an esoteric problem in quantum physics, promising no great fame or notoriety. But that pursuit led him to discover Black Holes.

Certainty is intuitive this way — the nagging dread that data is missing is a signal to commit to finding it. Mandates are discovered by paying attention to voids in subjectively meaningful data — the important path to all discovery in any field. Certainty exists, in great part, by virtue of the commitment to a path of data discovery, and to hell with the outcome. With outcome dependence, the prospect of such commitments can be fearfully debilitating. Mallory certainly understood the risks of the climb, especially after his first two attempts. He made the decision to demote potentially dangerous outcomes and promote his mandate, for which he paid with his life.

I had to decide that my understanding Certainty was worth the work. Certainty was the goal of my individual expedition, and it turned out that TCP provided a route-finding formula for me. In the same way an alpinist might adapt to altitude by repeated exposure to ever higher and more dangerous topography, my elevation to Certainty was only possible by habituating myself through repeated exposure over the abyss of uncertainty.

"I've always been about incremental progress; I mean it's funny because I've done maybe 35 first free solos. Really, when you lay them out, it's a long, long road that eventually culminated with El Cap…"

~ HONNALD,
ALEX HONNALD GOES UNDERCOVER ON THE INTERNET, 2020

Certainty is becoming accustomed, step by step, to confronting fear of the unknown, specifically fear of those influences that are beyond one's control. Mastering the skills that extend the limits of my control frees me from the infinite void of conditionals. Instead I focus energy on doing a few things well.

Certainty training is so hard initially because clinging to conditionals is so enticingly easy. After all, why master my life when it is so effortless to be the victim of it. But fear and regret always accompany dependency on externals, an unacceptable fate for me. Certainty is not being fearless. It is finally capitulation to the fatigue of allowing fear and uncertainty to be the driver of my decisions and actions. So, though my individual path may not work for you, TCP is a compass that may help you on your path.

For me, the deep sense of place and purpose it provides will be with me forever. If that sounds rather important, then perhaps you should read on. NΩ

GLOSSARY

The Certainty Principle	TCP is an equation that describes the relationship among five variables that determine the brain's state of certainty.
Certainty	Certainty is the brain-state of equilibrium, defined as confident optimism. Achievement increases with certainty.
Horizon	Horizon is an individual's temporal perspective, or decision-making time-frame of accountability. The quality and quantity of choices improve as horizons expand, compounding certainty.
Mandate	Mandate is an individual's locus of accountability. It is that unique domain of purpose that defines which tasks and problems have priority, and which should be avoided. An individual's definition of, and diligence to, a mandate builds certainty.
Income	Income is the aggregate of all benefits that accrue in the persistent execution of an individual's mandate. It is the underlying driver of mandate diligence, even in the face of failure. Monitoring and measuring incomes creates certainty.
Identity	Identity (or vanity) is the brain's fabricated story of itself. As a sorting device the brain is compelled to order experience relatively for survival. Sorting out its own existence is impossible. But the manifestation of its constant struggle to do so is the delusion called identity. Identity distorts experience and occludes opportunity, therefore it diminishes certainty.
Outcomes	Outcomes are produced by the confluence of individual choices of action, together with the external conditions within which these actions play out. Regret and fear result from the brain's enthrallment with past and future outcomes. Though actions create certainty, outcomes are probabilistic and are unreliable as a source of certainty creation.

CHAPTER 1
— MEETING DAVY CROCKETT —

1.1 – Davy and Me

"Dave, be sure you are right, then go ahead."
~ FESS PARKER / DAVY CROCKETT (PARKER, 1989)

Davy Crockett was one of the first TV miniseries. Produced by Disney, it aired in the mid-1950s, and re-ran again and again into the early '60s. Most boys of my generation were coonskin-cap wearing devotees of the legendary frontiersman portrayed by Fess Parker. I was no exception. Along with Elvis, the show, and its popular theme song, became male cultural icons of the day. As a kid my Mom's pet name for me became "Davy Crockett," after my legendary namesake, and it remained so right up to the time of her death.

Imagine my surprise when one day in 1989 while shopping at a Safeway grocery store in San Francisco (of all places), I'm rounding an end cap and walk right into 6'-5" Fess Parker standing in front of a display of wine bottles labeled Parker Estates. Though I was then a grown up, that didn't keep me from going stupid at the sight of my childhood hero. Well, I'm guessin' this wasn't the first time Ol' Fess had to suffer such silliness from someone over the age of 10. Af-

11

ter talking me back down to acting like an adult, he took a large card out of his pocket, asking me "What was your name again?" I had not introduced myself, but he autographed it along with the historically accurate Crockett quote.

TCP shows me that being sure I am right, then going ahead, doesn't promise that the outcome will turn out as expected. But at least I know where I am headed — and knowing where I am headed beats the alternative by a frontier mile.

Heads up, horizontal thinking reduces the perception of the inevitable obstacles on the path by creating the confidence to overcome or avoid them without getting stuck. The certainty that I will get myself out of pretty much whatever predicament I encounter means that I don't have to waste time and energy worrying about any particular outcome. Certainty comes in carelessness about outcomes. This might seem like circular logic, but what works for Davy is good enough for me!

At 10, my friends Chris and Taylor and I were pretty much the local chapter of the Davy Crockett Club. On weekends we were inseparable, and during the summertime especially, our vast frontier was the thousand acres or so surrounding my family's farm in southeast Pennsylvania. Our missions were simple — hiking and hunting crayfish and snakes and other critters while navigating the twin streams that ran through the lowlands of our frontier. We needled each other for sure, but we always felt that we, like Davy, were the good guys. Summer days were all Saturdays.

We'd meet up and go exploring with our bikes, our BB guns, our bows and Bowie knives along the endless deer trails that crisscrossed the fields and woods. We were limited only by how far we could hike before getting hungry. We'd meet under a hundred-foot Black Oak that stood roughly center-point of the triangle formed by our three houses. If I got there first,

I'd sprawl out in the grass and doze off, soaking in the summer around me. I felt planted, as deep as the oak roots running under my back. The daydreaming delight of gazing up through the leaves, waiting for the boys on one school-free June morning still sticks with me. Cutting a stalk of honeysuckle flowers, I dropped my gear and plopped down in the clearing to chew the sweet buds. The sun-soaked wind hissing through the wheat grass and across my face sent dizzying electricity through my head. I was free, and my anticipation of a day hiking into fresh adventures with my buddies was too good to be true. The possibilities seemed endless. Until the sun set over our barn, I'd be going. And armed with my bow and knife I was sure there was nothing on the trail that I couldn't deal with. I was immortal.

I wanted to keep the deep joy of being a kid set free from school and parental control, confident that wherever I went or whatever I found when I got there was going to be just fine with me. I've traveled to many exotic places since, and fragments of that feeling often return, but always a pale shadow of those extraordinary mornings back then. I've struggled with understanding why those days felt so perfect, and why my confident enthusiasm faded as I grew older.

That is, until I began investigating TCP. Until Mr. Bogle (below) wrote me in 2014 about "forever horizons." That expression evoked a refreshing feeling — that same "at-home-in-my-skin" confidence I'd known at 10. Did the experience suggest there was a formula for restoring and maintaining this optimistic confidence — this certainty? I decided I would find out. I would go hunting for the home I'd left many decades before.

"For the information of young hunters, I will just say that, whenever a fellow gets bad lost, the way home is just the way he don't think it is. This rule will hit nine times out of ten."
~ Crockett, 1834

Was it my preparation, the care for my gear, the chores completed and arriving early, that made my eagerness and confidence in the course of the day so authentic? Was it the trust we "Crocketteers" had perfected, back at a time when we chose our own way? How could I find my brain back to the place where the tall grass hisses and the wind electrifies, and stay there, forever. Could I find that place that holds the sensation of invincibility that I experienced as that summer boy of 10?

Discovering the secret for me — of why it all seemed so right that day, and why it all seemed so certain — came from just the opposite direction I was looking. Invincibility wasn't found reminiscing about the past. It was discovering that limitations tended to disappear when I discovered a deep understanding of my mission and an unlimited perspective about the future. That perspective unshackled me from identification with threats (prospective fear about the future) and regrets (retrospective fear about the consequences of past actions) that dogged me in my latter days. I could be a free man, free to be selfless. And selflessness is the starting place of Certainty. NΩ

Chapter 2
Physics of Certainty

2.1 — Pascal's Wager (A Dramatization)

The guiltless galaxy spins on in concert majesty,
Until at some appointed time,
Each note of it resigns,
To recompose in rhapsodies, even more sublime.
Why then should it be, much different for me?
For am I not that stuff from which stars are made?

As a logician, I had come to believe in the inevitable uncertainty of man's grasp of natural order of things. That is, until the fateful event recounted here, from which I expect never to recover my former despair of uncertainty.

Soon after midnight on the morning of Monday, 24 November 1654, I was driving my two-in-hand, returning our usual route from Nueilly to Paris by way of the Esplanade. Though I dressed for a more chilling return than my morning trip, I had loosened my neck scarf and removed my gloves. An unusually clement rain had moved through during the evening, warming and softening the cool air and washing the roadway slick. Late and exhausted, I pressed the team for home. I was as weary and as eager to reach my apartments in Saint Germain-des-Prés as was Virgil, my team lead, to return to his stable. Approaching the river, the dewy aired, but otherwise refreshing, drive suddenly thickened into a fog flowing up the banks, blanketing the road and us. The moonlight on which I relied to see vanished so quickly I was momentarily blind. But in my fatigue, I failed to slow the team, so confident was I in Virgil's command of the course, and so our speed exceeded the thin visibility. At once the team turned right, surging up the bridge ramp.   Gloveless, the slick reins slipped free and the team, heaving against the ramp, sent me backwards out of the seat as the wheels of the carriage skidded away across the wet rock. Though the events I am about to relate certainly transpired within no more than several seconds of time; I should note that the experience was protracted as if time itself had slowed to a point that I was observing a sequence of individual frames unfolding as paging through a child's picture book. Mounting the first arched section, 20 or 30 meters over the river, fear overwhelmed me as I grappled in the darkness at my feet for the reins. Just as I was rising back to my seat, fumbling to order the straps, Virgil lunged violently right again heading the team directly at the balustrade in the murk. In the next frame the brace reared up against the bridge wall spinning the carriage sideways. I could see with perfect clarity sparks rising slowly like soft lightening from his clad hooves, now dug deep into the Belgian stonework. Sailing past my face like snowflakes drifting and suspended, small chips of light showered up as the beasts struggled to halt their massive momentum. Uncanny is the only word that captures the fine detail of the unfolding in this terrible instant. Looking left there emerged from the fog an overturned peat wagon blocking the roadway, divert-

ing the team. The driver was standing before it waving his arms. This instant I could clearly see that his right hand bore a fresh wound, the torn flesh exposing a fragment of bone where his thumb once was. Again, I could inspect it in vivid detail from my seat suspended in this protraction. When confronting the wall, the poor beasts, more confused even than myself, reared to leap over it, oblivious that nothing but the river awaited them some 10 fathoms below. The front wheels of the carriage leapt with them, and at this mortal moment it seemed that the velocity of the event had slowed to an *arrêt de jeu*.

The lifting sensation terrified me, signaling the worst — that the entire rig, myself aboard, was vaulting into the abyss and a certain dreadful end. Yet, in that same instant, a powerful excitation surged through my body from my bones out. Dazzling and disorienting, I was seized by this terrible ecstasy. A sublime and strangely soothing sensation infused me, erasing the abject fear that had preceded it. Since the accident this sensation has periodically returned, and with even greater intensity, and that only adds to my confidence that the thought that accompanied it carried some primordial importance. It was the absence of all fear, a consuming force of calm and confidence, leaving in its wake an infusion of quietude and comfort like nothing I had formerly experienced. My perspective transformed to that of a bystander perfectly calm and detached from the events flickering past me. I had no investment in the outcome of the events. I watched as the horses' hooves, one by one, scraped over the marble capstone of the balustrade, disappearing sadly into the dark. Next the front wheels patiently splintered on the stonework as if under some fantastic weight that was ever so steadily and deliberately crushing them. I could see in amazing detail the destruction of it all. As the momentum lifted the carriage, the reins again yanked free with the horses fall and I could now peer over and just make out the trace which had broken away of the rigging and was tumbling in slow chaos towards the river. "Poor Virgil," I thought. It was at this instant, with the rear of the carriage rotating upwards, and the resignation that I was done for, that my insight occurred. As one who has spent months deliberating even the simplest mathematical problems, I am still bewildered that such a fantastic and comprehensive understanding of mind could be delivered whole and complete in a lightening flash. It was simply this:

> *"If God does not exist, one will lose nothing by believing in him, while if he does exist, one will lose everything by not believing."*
> PASCAL, PENSÉES, 1670

This insight I have since translated into its various implications both scientific and philosophical. But at the instant it occurred to me, as an ineffable understanding of the incredibly remote, yet distinct, probability of my own immortality, which I have reformulated as the following general rule of natural law:

> *"It is not certain, that all is uncertain."*
> PASCAL, TREATISE ON AIR PRESSURE, 1653

As in the Pascal's Wager story, things changed for me after uncovering the forever horizons principle. A little serious contemplation suggested that the consequences of my actions are permanently recorded in each instant seemed obvious enough. The probability, however remote, that my actions have indelible consequences was sobering, even frightening. Which is why, I imagine, so many have rebutted Pascal's Wager so passionately. Pascal was the rock-star mathematician of his day. His observations on the nature of certainty lead to probability theory which has influenced the course of mathematics and science for nearly four centuries. Fundamentally, Pascal's proposition that even the remote possibility that there is no avoidance of individual and perpetual accountability, challenges each to make the certainty choice of a lifetime.

2.2 — Conservation and Chaos

The science of comparative methods sheds some light on the validity of Pascal's Wager. Consider that the "physics" making up my physical self never escape reality because my body is literally the stuff from which reality is built. Each atom of me recycles into the macrocosm. What I am built of has been reformed infinite times through countless millennia from halfway across the galaxy. The transformations from form to form are constrained by the laws of chemistry and physics, deterministically. A time-lapse radiologic video map of a decomposing animal corpse provides conclusive (if somewhat revolting) evidence of this remarkable process.

If I am atomically perpetual, then what about the perpetuation of my actions? Do my choices map permanently into the "big picture," like the atoms that make up my body? In the context of cause and effect, the answer is undeniably "Yes." Regardless the religious implications of Pascal's Dilemma, the conclusion is regularly and secularly the same. Just as there is no escape from the physics of my physical being, my actions effect everything forever. So, if the laws of physics determine the course of my body's chemistry, what are the laws by which my choices are made, and does ignorance of my laws disadvantage me? "Yes," again! Mathematician Edward Lorenz's Chaos Theory, aka "The Butterfly Effect" (Lorenz, 1972), eloquently describes the calculus of this extraordinary relationship.

"... slightly differing initial states will evolve into considerably different states. If the flap of a butterfly's wings can be instrumental in generating a tornado, it can equally well be instrumental in preventing a tornado."

TCP recognizes that, just as the elements comprising my body will go on recomposing in the real world forever after me, so each of my actions are integrated into every subsequent instant, forever. To paraphrase Lincoln: "I will never escape history." NΩ

CHAPTER 3

— THE CERTAINTY PRINCIPLE —

My Horizon Forever
Manifest My Mandate
Account My Incomes
Surrender My Outcomes
Depose My Identity

3.1 — The Certainty Principle

"Man is a miracle."
MIRANDOLA G. P., 1486

Mirandola's "Dignity of Man" was the central philosophical manifesto of the renaissance period. Over less than a decade, his powerful defense of humanism would elevate the work of influential contemporaries and followers, including the Medici dynasty, Leonardo da Vinci, Michelangelo, and eventually Shakespeare, Descartes, Galileo, Newton, and other antecedents of the enlightenment period. Though condemned by the church, Pico defended the primacy of self-determination and free will until his death by poisoning in 1494.

Certainty is the supremacy of self-determination. Certainty is in the bones. But how do I reliably attain and sustain it? What is the formula for certainty? The Uncertainty Principle in physics establishes that the accurate determination of the position and momentum of objects is impossible, (Heisenberg W., 1927). What, then, can be said of the accurate determination of my place and motivations? Am I doomed to uncertainty? Many smart people think so?

21

> *"The whole problem with the world is that fools and fanatics*
> *are always so certain of themselves, and wiser people are*
> *full of doubts."*
> BERTRAND RUSSEL

Russel's intellectual platitude suggests that we should even doubt his own "wise" assertion about doubt. It may be accurate, but is it actionable? The Certainty Principle does not attempt find a solution to the certainty/uncertainty dilemma. TCP is the decision to rise above the dilemma. Mirandola' s "miracle" was an individual choice of what was certain for him. He could have just as well written that "Man is a mess." Likewise, I am compelled to choose, and I choose to elevate myself above my brain's divisive cognitive chaos, which is the very heart and cause of all uncertainty. Once I decided to view the world from beyond that mundane framework, I could see the five elements that make certainty scientifically accurate.

3.2 — $C = H^x \times M^x \times In / O^x \times Id$:
The Arithmetic of Certainty

Certainty increases as my horizon expands, as I act on my mandates and account my incomes, all the while diminishing

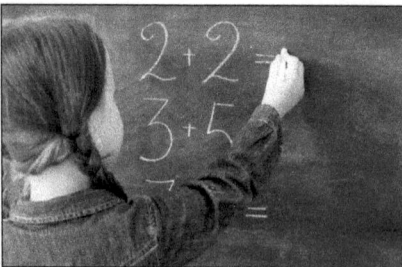

my identification with outcomes. Authorizing my identity to primary importance will occlude my horizon of achievement like a storm front, diminishing certainty. For certainty to prevail, I need to overcome the problem of outcomes getting stuck in my brain's identity filter. For example, getting fired or not getting a job or promotion can be devastating to my identity. So why rely on it? Identity free, I am in control, my horizons are unlimited, and I have the clarity to proceed with the duties mandated by my goals. With my horizon fixed in the distance, I can attend to the problems and tasks presented to me, unencumbered by the stories in my head.

The Certainty Principle (TCP) states that:

$$\text{Certainty} = \frac{\text{Horizon x Mandate x Incomes}}{\text{Outcomes x Identity}}$$

My sense of certainty (and confidence) is only limited by allowing outcomes and identity to dominate my long-term perspective on my purpose. If my horizon is short, and my preoccupation with my brain's story is great, I will be timid — unable to confront and take responsibility for the problems and opportunities that life constantly presents. If my horizon is vast, and I am free from a burdensome, time-and-energy consuming identity, I become confident and at ease with unfolding reality. In his book MAN'S SEARCH FOR MEANING, Viktor Frankl states: "Life ultimately means taking responsibility to find the right answers to its problems, and to fulfill the tasks which it constantly sets for each individual." (Frankl, 1946).

TCP tells me that I can optimize my performance, *if* my perspective is great enough and *if* I can learn to free myself from the nagging belief that I am anything other than the actions that I constantly take in addressing internal responsibilities. In the ALLEGORY OF THE CAVE (Plato, 380 BC), Plato shows us that it only requires an act of courage to climb "out of the cave" to recognize that these two achievements are really one in the same. There is factually no human reality outside of Frankl's mandate. We are only the instantaneous choices of action that we take — or fail to take — as they present themselves. That's it. It is simplicity itself. My identity — my stories — are merely illusions, merely shadows on the wall of the cave preventing me from seeing Plato's truth.

You are what you do, not what you identify with. Want power? Stop identifying with power and learn to evaluate and use the power you have effectively so that it grows. Want money? Let go of identifying yourself with money and learn the algebra of using money effectively to multiply itself.

So, what is the pay-off of the TCP formula? The sense of confidence and well-being that comes from freedom from fear and regret. The knowledge that regardless of the illusion of identity, nothing is impossible when horizons are forever. NΩ

CHAPTER 4

C IS FOR CERTAINTY

Certainty is not the absence of uncertainty; it is gaining the courage to relinquish attachment to uncertainty." (TCP)

"Courage is a kind of salvation."
PLATO, 380 BC

4.1 — Certainty and Courage

Certainty is a choice accompanied by a physical sensation in the bones. Human experience is at root, emotional. The emotional root of certainty is capitulation to courage because no other acceptable choice remains. It happens when I become sick and tired of the relentless harangues of fear and regret.

"Courage is the price that life exacts for granting peace."
EARHART, 1932

When preoccupation with fear and regret are finally abandoned, all that remains is courage. Certainty is the base human state where there is only courage. Courage isn't developed, it is always there, masked and distorted by my brain's enthrallment with uncertainty-driven vanity. When death comes, courage is all that remains, vanity stripped bare naked. Courage is inevitable, but meanwhile I can choose to suffer instead, avoiding the certain life.

When I was a kid, I was afraid of dangerous stuff. Hanging off cliffs, exploring caves, and trying to kiss Debbie Stewart topped the "this is going to kill me" list. Though they could have killed me (Debbie's Dad), they probably wouldn't have.

And relinquishing those experiences to fear makes my life all the poorer. Mustering oneself to the inevitability of freedom from mortality is a lesson best learned young.

Our forefathers and foremothers were more courageous because mortality was more apparent. They grew up with people and animals dropping dead left and right. Real death was common, so the skills for dealing with real life were common, too. My life is way more abstract. Death is mainly a story on TV. Digital engagement further abstracts reality, fomenting fear and regret.

At 10 life was raw. First-hand encounters with reality, the face-to-fist, the bloodied knee, the gasping for breath, generated feelings galvanizing the lessons learned and the courage accrued. As an adult, I can experience virtually, and virtual life is not the same thing. My "live-fire life" is being co-opted by my "virtual video life," insulating me from the courage-revealing suffering that was natural among those in the past who lacked my exposure to YouTube.

4.2 — Wantless

Needing is certain necessity. Wanting is vanity. Like the feeling in the gut when standing on the edge of a cliff, "getting" TCP happens in the body first in a way that the brain cannot get its head around. It is a sensation of wantless. Wantless is the liberation TCP delivers, the desire-free brain focused on what needs doing, what is mandated. The advantage and challenge of the TCP is abandoning my addiction to what I want, and investing in what I need instead. Wanting to lose weight makes me fat. Needing to lose weight, regardless the sacrifice, even if it kills me, makes me thin. The wanting mechanisms are simply bad habits established over years of practice, so discerning wants from needs is hard at first. I overcome it by creating the new habit of dismissing my wants. If a decision or action is not in service to my mandate, I need to dismiss it. If I don't know my mandate, I must stop wanting one. If I pay close attention, I will notice when it sneaks up and jumps into my lap.

> *"As soon as you stop wanting something, you get it."*
> ANDY WARHOL

"Wanting" is just the brain-rapping that often haunts most waking hours. Replacing it with needing promotes reality over illusion. Sure, my brain invariably worms its way back in to solve problems, manage tasks, and abstract stories. But with practice, certainty comes to dominate, because learning to experience undistorted reality delivers better outcomes than deferring to delusion. TCP is galvanized by programming the brain with the five elements of certainty. This "feedback loop of certainty" grows increasingly comfortable and productive as horizons become ever more expansive and mandates dominate.

Once certainty rules, my brain's rightful place as a problem-solving device is restored, and I utilize it mostly as a reasoning tool, rather than the over-dominant, identity-seeking vanity master of every waking moment. Wantlessness is the biggest psychological payoff of the TCP mindset. When I require logical analysis, I call on my brain's reasoning services. But certainty masters my brain, my brain no longer masters me.

4.3 — Codifying Certainty
What goes to words gets done.

Close your eyes and think back to a moment in your life when you felt the sensation of certainty. Of being confidently and optimistically at home in your bones. A deep sense of belonging right where you were, doing exactly what you were supposed to be doing. Visualize the place. What kind of day was it? Try recalling the events that led up to the experience. Were you alone? If not, who was with you? Try re-experiencing the letting-go-ness of it, like dropping in an elevator. That instance of invincibility. Freedom from the furrowing forehead, from jaws judgmentally clenched in defense, shoulders surrendered, slackened, and relaxed. Perhaps a sky-wide sigh of satisfaction so deep it was intoxicating. Like the warmth of saturating sunlight after a long damp night wind blowing down your neck. A feeling of being loose and ready for anything. The uncanny feeling of belonging. A rightness in the gut so authentic that you know your home. How did it feel? Was there a settling, like all the puzzle pieces falling into place? A sense of elation? Perhaps waves of warm electricity running through your body and skull that felt so powerfully primordial, that while unfamiliar could only originate from the physics of the instant.

Sure, words are abstractions of real experience. But for much of experience, words are good enough to power a plan of action. (As we will see, words create action and reality itself.) The deepest sensations are almost ineffable, but, fortunately, almost is enough when it comes to choosing the important direction forward.

"And most important, have the courage to follow your own heart and intuition. They somehow already know what you truly want to become. Everything else is secondary."
JOBS, 2005

Though a sense of certainty is important, the diligence of writing it in words is the tough and necessary task for making it real and lasting. The brain's binary-linear process requires the connection of dots to extrapolate next decisions and next actions. Whereas a lack of attention, focus, and diligence cause uncertainty, meticulous "recor-necting" (i.e., recording and connecting) of specific data points reveals the way to value. Creating certainty is hard work, and starting off this work can be frustrating and discouraging. The path to certainty stumbles, falls, and hurts. But the alternatives of vanity — regret, fear, and desperation, even insanity — make it worth the work.

Once I accept that certainty requires the happy acceptance of struggle, the work of formulating it begins to become easier because certainty diminishes the relative significance of suffering. Consider my over-reactive whining when, for example, my home internet goes down. Then compare that to something genuinely painful and uncertain, like Frankl's incarceration. Certainty keeps "hurt feelings" in scaled perspective with true suffering.

With practice, keeping track and keeping score of my choices and outcomes becomes an unconscious competence that breeds achievement. The work itself enriches my horizons and compels me to act on my mandates. Persistence writing into reality establishes a path to the achievement that is otherwise impossible. Hence the cure for cancer, the end of hunger, the Turing Test, and the solo ascent of K2 will all be achieved on paper before they become reality. This is the fundamental mechanics of important human achievement. Frank Smythe, after an early attempt on Everest, captured the spirit of this rule while emphasizing the necessity for detailed route planning prior to the climb.

"Perhaps it is not too much to say that Everest will be
climbed in England."
SMYTHE, 1934

4.4 — A Picture of Certainty

One early June morning I stood at the edge of the field above
our rural farm in southeastern Pennsylvania. I was 11. I'd fin-
ished my chores, and with a belly full of sugar-loaded Chee-
rios, I was heading out to meet my two best buddies, Chris
and Taylor. Our plan was bow shooting at an old sand dump
sitting atop the big hill in the field half mile above my house.

I carried my old Black Bear
English long bow over my
shoulder, a quiver full of field
arrows, and a Buck knife on
my belt. I'd wet-proofed my
Red-Wings with linseed oil,
and laced them up snake
high. My jean pockets were
stuffed with Chum-Bubble
Gum and best of all, I had
passed the 5th grade! I was
a free man set for anything.
I felt a rush of invincibili-
ty. What a great feeling! As I marched up the hill there was
no thought of next year or next week or even tomorrow. Age
meant nothing much and school seemed forever away. I was
reading Jack London's CALL OF THE WILD, and I was about to
set off on an adventure with two guys I trusted with my life.

"There is an ecstasy that marks the summit of life, and beyond
which life cannot rise. And such is the paradox of living,
this ecstasy comes when one is most alive, and it comes as a
complete forgetfulness that one is alive."
LONDON, 1903

No secrets. No judgments. Fearlessly one for all, and all for one. We were the Three Musketeers, and we loved playing the part. Everything seemed to be exactly as it was supposed to be — right place, right time, with an unlimited supply of "Hey, let's go for it" possibilities.

This is a word picture of certainty. But why so certain? What was it that made our adventures in blood brotherhood so liberating? Well, I never wore a watch. When the shadows got long it was time to head home. When I'd finally fall into bed, I never checked a clock, I was too tired for time. I had no sense of my own mortality. Falling off the barn roof, dangling from the bridge beams, shredding myself in a bike crash were always followed with, "Whatever you do, don't tell Mom."

I feared her more than bloody shins or broken ribs. Fear, when it did happen, lasted for the instant it took to grab a pinned water snake, drop it into a coffee can and slap down the lid, followed by the Davey Crockett theme playing over and over in my head. My duties were simple and clear: cleaning my rifle, feeding the chickens, being a buddy, and never, ever doing my schoolwork. Just reading and rereading CALL OF THE WILD without writing a book report. Never fearing if I could handle whatever trouble presented itself along the trail. If I couldn't manage, my pals would help me out. Finally, I had no sense of some special me that I had to live up to. There was little need for checking about the right or wrong thing to do. I had heroes for that, Crockett and the Lone Ranger. I carried a buck knife and a rifle just like Davey, and like the Masked Man taught me, "To have a friend, you must be a friend." What else did I really need to know about myself? I wasn't Davey. I was just a kid playing Crockett, but I loved the part. Whenever balking at another dumb, death-defying double-dare, all it took to turn this frighten kid into a frontier fighter one more time was Chris poking me, "Hey, what's a matter, Davey Crockett? Ya scared?"

In thousands of hours consulting and coaching, my conversations with clients always focus on helping them improve their sense of confidence about choices of action (or inaction), and helping to correctly solve the problems, or complete the tasks mandated by their business and professional objectives. Delivering confidence lead me to formulate a coaching process focused on how confidence worked. A rich vein of self-confidence, tempered by regular reality-testing, leads to successful outcomes. That was my theory. But I found that confidence alone wasn't enough. Authentic self-confidence came from someplace personal and deep, often forged by important challenges confronted and overcome. Confidence came at the price of a resignation to having to figure it out on paper.

For example, it's easy to lose perspective about which fights matter, and which fights should be abandoned without a strategy. I've worked with confident people who were so sure of themselves they couldn't let go of the bad habits that sabotaged their success. I've worked with otherwise confident clients who struggled with accountability. Consistently recognizing, planning, and executing against priority problems and tasks was problematic. Then there were others who were confident but dogmatic and simply uncoachable. They had trouble listening and learning. Their vanity so dominated their values that conflicting viewpoints were reflexively perceived as threats, triggering a fight response. Their thoughts and ideas had become central elements of a well-defended personal identity that had built itself up in their brains over years of reinforcement. The most disturbing part of these insights was that I knew someone intimately who suffered from all these vulnerabilities. That person was me!

The special confidence formula I was seeking had to encompass all three:

- self confidence born of a long-term perspective,
- mandated self-accountability, and
- an immunity to vanity-based identity.

It seemed that perspective, judgment, and a unique lack of self-consciousness also played a part in the art of confident optimism. So, I looked for a better word, and a better formula.

Certainty is the physical sensation of confidence — knowing I am in the right place, doing the right thing. Certainty requires momentum — moving forward with an attitude of limitless possibility. Certainty is being comfortable in my own skin that unique sensation of action well-grounded. I decided that certainty was my holy grail, and perpetuating such a state was my goal. I realized that uncertainty was merely an artifact of my brain's cognitive processes, not the natural state of me. The natural state came first. My brain was just a problem-solving tool for navigating reality. But it wasn't me. In effect, there never was an uncertain me. Where I was, certainty was. I just needed to crack the code. **NΩ**

CHAPTER 5
——THE SCIENCE OF CERTAINTY——

I knew scientifically that uncertainty was the native state of reality — wasn't it? Uncertainty had been established as a principle of physics by Heisenberg nearly 100 years ago. HEISENBERG, 1927

$$\partial x \partial p \geq \frac{1}{2\pi} h$$

Math aside, Heisenberg proved that simultaneous position and momentum measurements of an object is always uncertain. To translate this into TCP terms, the accurate determination at any instant of where I am (my situation) and what I am doing (my action) are impossible. The brain cannot handle what I "am" and what I "do" simultaneously. It's one or the other. This is the fundamental human cognition problem. When I focus on where I stand, action is lost. When I focus on action, my position is lost. TCP agrees with TUP. To achieve Certainty, I need to be looking at one or the other, separately and subjectively.

First define my situation, where I am (S_1) and where I want to be (S_2), and then determine the sequential action steps (A_n) required to get me there.

$$S_2 - S_1 = \Sigma \, (A_1 + A_2 + A_3 + A_n...)$$

Intuitively I understood that the variables within my absolute control were limited. The outcomes of my actions were always dependent to some degree on external conditions that were beyond my influence. After all, though I can use an umbrella, I cannot stop the rain. The world, according to modern science, was probabilistic. So where was Certainty to be found in this model? Not in any particular outcome, but in the logistical structure, the plan of actions for getting from one place to another, just as I would plan a trip with a map. Fundamentally, Certainty is planning and executing irrespective of any particular Outcome, other than (as in an experiment) the value the data the outcome provides.

5.1 — Outcomes vs. Incomes

My Outcomes have probabilities. My Incomes are elemental to the results of my actions, the real data. Certainty accrues with the knowledge that the measures of my Incomes, over time, are the measure of mandate excellence. Like smelting iron ore, Certainty renders incomes that are free of the identity-supporting "slag" that can attach itself to experience. But outcomes are not independent of incomes. Every result comes with a story. So how to develop the skills for right decision making to optimize, but not attach to, the outcomes of my subsequent actions? The more complete my knowledge of a system, and the more skillful I am as a result, the more accurate and precise my incomes and the more control I have over my rendering of the outcomes I experience. When I was building my go-cart, I had no idea what I was doing, and the outcome reflected my ignorance. I crashed less as I learned more, but I still crashed occasionally.

But domain of control alone does not deliver Certainty because outcomes are still probabilistic. I also needed to master my response to outcomes. Certainty includes both. Certainty is optimizing control over the variables in my domain of accountability while understanding that outcomes always include variables out of my control. Certainty was the combination of right actions and, more importantly, the right attitude that the results of those right actions were to a greater or lesser degree independent. More certain about my actions, coupled with my greater freedom from the influence of outcomes, meant I was becoming liberated from the tyranny of uncertainty.

Perpetuating that sensation of Certainty became my mission. But what was the underlying science of it? In business, certainty describes those conditions that promote capital investment and growth. Investing requires clarity. But clarity itself comes in two parts: a well-defined goal on the horizon plus an unambiguous and undistorted view of the path for getting there. What principles generate such a perspective? What practice would establish an action bias? What habits of mind would have to be abandoned? What poor behaviors encumbered learning and judgment, preventing a clear view of what was important and what could be left behind? Perhaps a closer look at the science will reveal some clues.

5.2 — Certainty is the Compass of Biological Life

Certainty is the vector of life. As we will see, whether people or paramecium, certainty is the path forward toward a compelling goal, but not any particular outcome on that path. Stock markets rise and fall in accordance with the aggregate certainty as perceived by buyers and sellers, up or down. Choices of action are amended or vetoed altogether by the level of certainty about the probable outcomes of such actions. The dating habits of humans is a ritual dance wherein the threat of rejection can paralyze or propel the actor, contingent purely on their level of certainty about the outcome. Science has examined the origins of such behavior. If we look closely enough, we can see that the human struggles with identity-based behavior map from the basic survival instinct fundamental to all life on earth.

My Paramecium Brain: Origins of Uncertainty

Survival is the source of all emotion. No living thing exists without it. A paramecium placed in a tube with varying concentrations of sugar solution behaves neurotically. The bug will begin random spinning each time it encounters a drop in the concentration of a sweet glucose snack. In a simplified model, the bug's survival system rewards it with a little chemical "boost" of serotonin* when it finds itself swimming in the direction of more sugar. So it keeps going in that direction. However, should the sugar concentration fall, its little legs paddle furiously, causing it to spin in search of a higher density of glucose molecules. This random spinning behavior repeats until it detects more sugar, at which point it stops, reverting to linear paddling and continuing on its merry way until encountering another sugar shortage. The paramecium "brain" compares successive samples, triggering a spin response when the concentration falls. So long as the receptors respond "yes" to the glucose bias of the successive samples, the direction of motion is unchanged. A "no" signal from the concentration test triggers a spinning routine that eventually redirects forward motion. This phenomenon of chemotaxis (Adler, 1974) works in reverse when the critter encounters a repellent — spinning randomly in search of relief from stuff it deems disgusting.

---

* Serotonin is evolutionarily conserved across the animal kingdom.

Similarly, my human brain responds to reality based on how it serves my highly evolved, abstracted survival instinct. It's abstract because the human brain has extrapolated the meaning of survival and its related attractants and repellents far beyond mere metabolic value. Humans are herd animals, and acknowledgment of my identity by my group is the second most powerful human motive, behind physical survival. (Bion, 1961). As modern man, my "spinning" is seldom based on a threat to physical survival (fight or flight) as much as the ongoing challenges to the survival of my identity. My "instinct" for identity survival becomes a perpetual battle with the conditional elements (externals, thus not in my control) of experience. It is a no-win contest. Like the paramecium, I get shots of serotonin and dopamine that sooth my brain when conditions are identity-sustaining. But cortisol (stress) and adrenaline (fear, flight) when my identity is threatened or defeated. Consider the physiology when my favorite sports team or political candidate suffers a loss. As the meaning of my identity is challenged by the defeat, the fight or flight response results as the brain's dopamine receptors become flooded with adrenaline, (Bo Xing, 2016). Consider, rabid fans of opposing sports teams who become aggressive, even violent, when team identification is threatened by the loss of an important match. The threat to the survival of vanity causes cognitive chaos. Like the paramecium's sugar dance, my brain spins in search of identity-reinforcing inputs, and if I can't find them, I might seek validation through a punch in the mouth. My identity-reliance constantly seeks perceptions that inflate it and attacks, or avoids, those that threaten it, along with the commensurate emotional jolt. And it's that jolt that matters. Left unchecked, attachment to the "emotional fix" that are triggered by identity "attractants and repellents," becomes addictive, even maddening! Consider chronic depression, when spinning for identity reinforcement turns into a spiraling abyss — not for lack of meaning, but because the object of meaning can never be "self" because "self," *per se*, is pure fabrication. It does not exist.

UC Berkeley's Dan Koshland's (Koshland & Sanders, 1989) experiments in the chemotaxis of motile organisms investigated this strange behavior pattern that vectored the paramecium away from repellents and towards attractants, deducing survival as the driver. But what is survival? Koshland discovered that behavior is triggered by a chemical process starting at the cell wall. If, as the paramecium moves along, its nose (cell membrane) goes off the scent (encounters fewer and fewer sugar molecules) the survival instinct kicks in, causing the creature to spin.

The principle of biological generalization (Darden, 1996) suggests that the behavior of more sophisticated organisms (e.g., humans) map from similar feedback mechanisms seen in the humble single-celled paramecium. Could it be that human behaviors are fundamentally driven by involuntary biochemical feedback systems mapped from this primordial template? Perhaps the emotion associated with vanity is simply a "feel good" biochemical infusion (i.e., serotonin and dopamine) caused by a sequence of self-justifying sensory data.

Learning that Brad Pitt wears the same brand of underwear that I do (I actually have not a clue on this topic) reinforces my identity. Therefore, I have a celebrity's "endorsement."

On the other hand, I have a choice when confronted with a challenge. Vilifying Bernie Sanders as evil because his political views differ from mine reinforces my self-image. After all, I must be good if Bernie is evil. This reaction is less threatening to my identity than confronting the reality that Bernie is a perfectly fine fellow, just like me, who just happens to be a socialist. TCP argues that when my brain construes data to be coherent with my identity (Bernie is evil), it is chemically reinforced. Any input that threatens vanity has the opposite effect, causing my brain to flail about in anxiety, fear, and regret. I call this effect "Vanitaxis" which, like chemotaxis, is the "spinning" caused by the pain of any data that even sniffs of a challenge to identity. It is less biochemically "painful" to construct a vanity-preserving story in identity defense than confronting the reality that my identity is flawed. Over time, such defensiveness becomes automatic, reflexively distorting reality to preserve my vanity's status quo.

5.2.1 — Reflexivity and "Vanitaxis"

If, as with the paramecium, human anxiety is triggered when reality conflicts with my identity, what can I do about defeating the reality-distorting effects of angst? Vanity-based

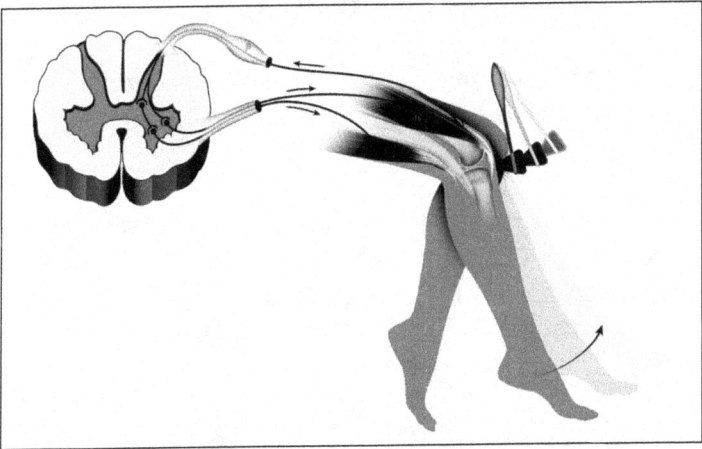

choices are reflexive. They lack consideration. Here I distinguish reflexive (vanity-based) behavior from rational behavior, which is based on, say, a rational strategy. Bundling up to attend a cold winter football game is rational behavior. Stripping down to the skin at the same game to affect an impression, albeit entertaining, is reflexive behavior based in identity seeking. Identity is reflexive, and the actions I take to preserve it are rooted in the same bug-brained binary algorithms as the paramecium. Preserving identity is little more than chemotaxis raised to the level of my vanity's survival contract. Vanitaxis is the compulsion to construe reality data to be self-reinforcing. Am I so conditioned by being rewarded with acknowledgment of my own identity that I am trapped in the "vanity tube" like the paramecium? Without TCP I am little more than a tiny creature swimming in a tube filled with a gradient of identity gratification, within which my brain has been conditioned to "spin" when unvalidated. Biology dictates the I will always suffer for nutrients and, therefore, seek air, water, and food. But to escape the "test tube" of identity requires a courageous leap to free myself from the confines of the reality-distorting identity survival contract that I reflexively seek to reinforce.

5.3 — Breaking My Identity Contract

> *"Man is born free; and everywhere he is in chains…*
> *I prefer liberty in danger than peace with slavery."*
> ROUSSEAU, 1762

I am a herd animal. My identity is the vitally human tonic note of the rhapsody of social survival. There is safety in herds (evidence any PBS "Nature" video about tuna or zebra).

Physical survival that dominates the primitive (amygdala) brain gave way to ever-greater abstraction of the survival instinct. Priorities attributed to survival evolved to become more sophisticated. The strains and struggles of day-to-day life are referred to as the survival. But what, precisely, is the modern human seeking to survive? Facebook?

As I lay dying, what am I really clinging to? Man makes monuments and temples, creates foundations, endowments, and various other memorializations to perpetuate identity and those with whom we identify. In and of themselves, that's not necessarily bad. But the fundamental motive goes beyond the physical. It is survival of the illusion of identity. Stripped of the trappings of our identity and our social queues, conveniences, and pleasantries, what then? In a post-apocalyptic world of true scarcity, what dictates behavior? The "Survivor" television show provides an artificial glimpse into such lean circumstances. We get a glimpse into what happens when people are placed into a synthetic dog-eats-dog scenario. Turns out, in a dog-eats-dog situation, identity is the first course!

I respond to reality largely due to the programming of billions of cultural conditionings, ported through my senses into my brain from birth. The source code is parental, familial, communal, and post-puberty feeds from peer groups and powerful marketing influences. In the aggregate, the instructions constitute my social contract — one that is pervasive and powerful. Reflexive compliance is so embedded in my brain's operating system that it defines the experiential boundary of day-to-day reality. Try radically changing the way you dress and cut your hair. Try changing the type of people you associate with. Try changing to a completely different career. As trivial as these changes might seem on paper, the first-hand fear generated by contemplation of these identity-breaks conjures from decades under the tyranny of a social contract steeped in vanity.

This contract remains intact unless I am forced, or force myself, to amend it through naked exposure to reality of what is or what must be, as dictated by my values. Getting fired for not fitting-in (I'd really rather be doing other work) is just such a Darwinian cause, compelling me to restructure the career part of the contract if I have the willpower and courage to seize the opportunity to do so. The shock of such an event offers up a chance, albeit temporarily, to break the pattern. These opportunities to escape the unconscious compliance with my legacy contract are rare and valuable. Without exposure to radical reality, either by my will or against it, the brain seeks to preserve its homeostatic routine. If I am a misfit, this can mean years of quiet prevaricating desperation.

Travel in unfamiliar lands confronts my contract, potentially initiating new perspectives, even changes, if my vanity allows it. Investigating new realms of thinking challenges the contract, compelling it to change. But the courage to journey is not enough! I can journey to simply reinforce my old prejudices supporting my identity, i.e., my existing social contract. Or I can journey out with the defined purpose of challenging and changing because I just can't stand my status quo anymore. The latter is the domain of TCP. The challenge is clinging to identity, which is the definition of vanity. If I am truly courageous, of the Ferdinand Magellan class, I must come to terms with the possibility that I may be radically, even fundamentally changed by the experience of exploration. I may discover madness or my own mortality just over the next horizon of my deepest convictions. But the intrepid traveler fears ignorance and delusion more than they fear their own mortality. This is the importance of the identity challenge. Abandoning identity is the great capitulation.

If this mortality motive is only a manifestation of the human identity, what is the fundamental cause? What if the underlying energy driving me to human actuality supersedes even the life and death struggle? After all, soldiers face death, sometimes even happily. With a 1-in-5 chance of not returning, climbers continue to challenge the dangerous summit of Nepal's Nanga Parbat in the Karakorum mountains. What is this motive that is greater than survival of self and life? What does it look and feel like? Would it even be definable in human cognitive terms?

5.4 — Wanting vs. Needing

My brain is a wanting machine. Dan Koshland's work in chemotaxis (Koshland & Sanders, 1989) essentially examines the primordial nature of "needing." One might say that needing is a fundamental qualification for an organism of any kind. "Needing" is a life-or-death necessity. There's no choice about it happening. You either do it or you die, physically or figuratively. In contrast, "wanting" is about gratification, a vanity-based motivation. A "need" presents few choices and many challenging consequences (sickness, death?). A "want" is an easier path because it lacks accountability. There are many choices, and the consequences are few and easily dismissed.

> *"You can't always get what you want.*
> *You can't always get what you want.*
> *But if you try sometime,*
> *You might find,*
> *You get what you need."*
> M. JAGGER/K. RICHARDS, 1968

Chemotaxis is driven by the needing of nutrients. Vanitaxis is driven by wanting what inflates identity. Unlike needing, which demands action, wanting is a chronic state in and of itself. Wanting to lose weight is a vanity-driven epidemic enabling a relentless onslaught — a schizophrenia of info-mercials about weight loss and cooking stuff. Almost anyone earning a passing grade in high school biology knows that carbohydrates are stored as fat. Yet 39 percent (OECD, 2017) of American adults are obese, and many more overweight. But Frito Lay's sales are doing just fine, thank you. Wanting is not needing, and the pursuit of vanity is wanting the impossible. The obesity epidemic is believed to be strongly related to another epidemic, the narcissistic preoccupation with self (Lemaitre, 2016). Effectively, seeking to inflate my identity makes me fat. So long as I identify with wanting to diet (someday maybe), my brain believes it is dieting. The problem is solved, and I forgo the willpower to take the required actions otherwise necessitated by needing. When I am needing to lose 30 pounds (it's life or death) the brain won't quit until it finds the way — at least those brains that prioritize living over death by gluttony. People who need to lose weight will go to extremes, even banding their stomachs to stop eating. Smokers who want to quit smoking, junkies who want to stop shooting heroin, people who want to escape dead-end jobs, and people who want to be wealthy will never achieve those things until they stop identifying with the want and begin acting on the need.

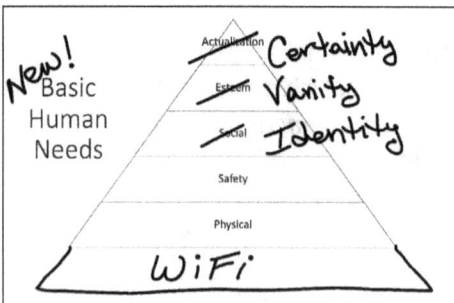

Crucial to certain living is building the capacity to either kill off my wants (the large majority) or make the decision to elevate a want to a need and do it fast, (meaning without thinking about it too much because the brain can rationalize away even the most virtuous decision). TCP teaches that needing a life-or-death commitment to a mandate manifests goals and creates momentum. Wanting does the opposite. It confuses and corrupts goals, creating inertia. So, one TCP key is to void wants as quickly as possible. Wanting is an identity-inflating, energy-consuming waste of human resources. To fight the "Wanting Demon," I must learn to demote those interests that don't serve my mandated needs, and quickly and consciously eliminate them. Popular media are parasites of want, and do everything in their power to play to my identity through them. Consider the editorial mandate of most news programming — "If it bleeds, it leads" — appealing directly to the identity-driven phenomenon of *schadenfreude*, i.e., — deriving pleasure, joy, or self-satisfaction from learning of, or witnessing, the troubles, failures, or humiliation of others. I wanted to watch TV news, but I understood it is little more than an identity-milking money machine. It did little but demotivate and distract, so I cut the cable.

Needing is commitment to action. Mindlessly muddling along accumulating wants may make my identity feel heavy and valuable, but it ends in slow death by dissipation. My meaningful life requires something in my life to have genuine, bedrock meaning. I might like Bruce Springsteen's music, and it is certainly important to Bruce, but really it is meaningless to me. The only music that can ever really matter to me is the music I make myself, even if it lacks Springsteen's rich poetic drumbeat of dead-end, desperation. Better to commit myself to accomplishing just one thing and failing; than a life of gratifying the gluttony of wants that serve my identity.

Warning! I am not suggesting that wanting is a benign condition. Wanting destroys certainty. Chronic wanting, like any addiction, disenfranchises the individual, opening a vein to infection by fear and regret. So, there is really no choice. Either I commit to my mandated needs, or I live in a world of wanting.

5.5 — The Uncertainty Organ

The brain escapes the instant. It is the organ and the origin of uncertainty. The brain creates the illusion of change through its capacity for abstraction, for escaping accuracy of instantaneous experience. Abstracting is the imaginary non-instant state that we refer to as past and future, made up of thin traces of images, sounds, emotions, and the words we use to conveniently organize our brain traces. I am not calling them memories, because computers have co-opted the term memory as a nearly perfect bit-for-bit digital reconstruction of reality. No, my brain lacks such accuracy. Try recalling today's breakfast accurately. What did it taste like, look like? At best, my recall is a thin trace. Curiously, even if an action is habituated, i.e., repeated over and over until it becomes a habit, I find it difficult to recount it accurately, point for point without careful study of the process and writing it down *ad nauseam*. If I try to consider a detailed chronology of my typical morning routine for example, I may find it quite difficult. The brain seeks novelty, doing its duty by processing new data and focusing on the fresh stuff. The only way to keep the brain gratified is by fresh action taken when it signals it is being confronted with a pattern incongruency — something that doesn't fit its multitude of cognitive templates. It signals me to wash my hands when my hands are in a state that is incongruent with its benchmarks for cleanliness. I barely need to think about it.

We further abstract these traces by labeling them with words — fundamentally sounds and symbols that represent the traces so we can capture some record of them. I might brand a Clapton concert as "moving" or "spectacular". But the words are themselves defined by other words, abstractions of abstractions, and fail to adequately capture the sensation when hearing the first seven notes of "Layla" (Clapton & Gordon, 1971). Without caution, so much brain abstraction distances my attention from authentic experience of the instant. A group dancing enthusiastically at a concert has an intense shared manifesting experience in the instant that is barely sharable later. King's "I have a dream . . ." and Kennedy's "Don't ask what your country can do for you . . ." speeches have echoed powerfully through the decades, inspiring many. But if you could ask someone who was in attendance what it was like hearing it, they might be rendered speechless. It's impossible to find the words that convey the instantaneous sensation of an epiphany. But without the words there is no communication of such traces to others or even reinforcement within the confines of my own brain. All sense of past and future is simply a brain-based trace, plus the cognitive abstractions it creates, digesting each trace through language and conceptualization — quite insubstantial compared with reality, and only gaining permanence after my brain creates an emotion validating it as important.

5.6 — Brain-Data Domain

The brain synthesizes certainty with emotion. It combines the traces of meaning with present sensory input, while adding a dash of emotion to make it "sticky" and *voilà*, new memory synthesis. Without the emotion there is no recall. Experiences lacking novelty skip emotional labeling, becoming habituated — pigeon-holed after regular exposure causing them to disappear into the background. Consider the daily commute or tooth brushing. Like the vivid foreground in the aerial perspective of a misty day, only traces with an emotional link are easily accessible. Emotion is effectively the brain's file labeling system. If the brain doesn't emotionally label an event, it disappears. Conversely, a highly emotional event can be indelible, even inescapable, regardless of my will to erase it.

As I age the emotionality of external experience wanes, as many common events are relegated to habituation. The novelty numbs. The emotion-laden traces from the past, however, remain imprinted, even photographically. Consider the sensation when I consider the phrase "my mother." It provokes an instantaneous emotional experience, combined with images and some associated words (abstractions of experience). Speaking the phrase "my mother" is merely a symbolic representation, a sound made by the vocal cords to represent a trace. But this familiar sound is over-laden with powerful emotions. Why do I reflexively recall my personal story of my mother tending to a bee sting on my foot when I was three, rather than the purely logical response that the symbol "mother" means one that gives birth to offspring? Why the conflation? Why the persistent algorithm of fitting reality into a preconceived story? Because story is abstraction of a trace of reality wrapped in emotion, and emotions create motive. Emotions are my root motivation to act. Call it "emotivation."

Though the brain appears to be my only domain of perception, it is not. Still, it is dominated by the senses. Eyesight is limited to the individual's visual bandwidth of electromagnetic (EMR) radiation, a function of the physics of the eye. But EMR goes infinitely beyond the visual range of humans. Hearing is limited to an individual's auditory range of frequencies, a function of ear mechanics. But sound frequencies range far beyond the human auditory spectrum. A CPU (central processing unit) set-up for iOS (Apple) cannot effectively process Windows, and vice versa. Likewise, I am limited to the scope of experience by my cognitive bandwidth, both intellectually (IQ) and systemically (cognitive binary source coding).

Let's call Bandwidth + IQ (B+IQ) the total human capacity for brain-based experience. This is to say 1.) that the brain is limited to a binary logic system, and 2.) just as each person has different visual acuity, each incidence of this brain system (e.g., my brain) is further constrained by its comprehensive intelligence capacity. Since my brain, it would appear, is the only conduit through which all my experience flows, my experience of reality is constrained, accordingly, by my B+IQ. Presumably, all my experiences of reality are bottle-necked and filtered by my B+IQ. In this context, I am a fish in the water of my B+IQ. So, knowing nothing but water, I have no context for air. All experience comes to me through my unique B+IQ. If there is a reality beyond, how can I experience it? Here's where the fish has the advantage. Because fish have minimal identity. But I am human with a brain big enough to seek self-justification. Adding it up, the potential limitations of human experience of reality can become manifold, unless I can control identity seeking. I am conditioned to know the instant of reality narrowly through my B+IQ, which is further distorted as it passes through the lens of the identity game. Whether or not I have an awareness that I am in the game is key.

Flying fish know there are experiences beyond the water. Their forefathers liked it so much they kept jumping until they evolved wings, enabling them to spend more time in the air. Likewise, with me. Once I recognize that my identity is a small game being played within a much larger and interesting domain, I will keep leaping beyond my identity.

In every way, then, such prisoners would recognize as reality nothing but the shadows of those artificial objects. How could they see anything but the shadows if they were never allowed to move their heads?
PLATO, 380 BC

Consider a domain of a slightly larger scope than my identity-based brain alone can conjure. What would that be like? Perhaps it has a horizon of possibility that is somewhat greater than my conventional identity will allow. Perhaps my brain is just a tool, a logistical device for solving problems and reasoning out next steps — important, but no longer the puppet master constantly spinning its narrative and pressing me to perform within that narrative. In this domain I free my thoughts from the constant anchor of identity-reinforcement. Like the flying fish, I am freed to evolve to this new horizon of possibilities. Failures and other impediments are diminished because I no longer seek identity meaning in them. Meaning, in effect, is not so meaningful. Like a first visit to Disneyland, this fantastic new domain relieves me of the compulsion to find identity in the experience. I am liberated from my identity allowing my childlike imagination to take over. As my old identity shrinks in the rear-view mirror, I am free to gaze alertly forward at what adventure is coming next. As I do, my reliance on anchoring my experiences in my identity dissolves in favor of simply discovering and responding to the larger world manifesting before my eyes. Likewise, the distance, the difficulties, and the disorders along the path are seen for what they really are, merely set pieces in a much larger game of limitless possibility. What is the scope of achievement available to me in this new domain? How grand could this new horizon become? What are the new destinies I can play at manifesting?

It turns out that the specific answers to these questions are, at the same time, both simple to see and hard to implement. Simple, because, set free of identity, my horizon of possibilities begins to expand and clarify. Hard because I must choose a course of action and stick to it without attaching identity to any particular outcome while using the real data from those outcomes as my compass. I must connect the dots. NΩ

CHAPTER 6

H IS FOR HORIZON:
── MY HORIZON IS FOREVER ──

"Never forget, your horizon is forever."
BOGLE, THE BOGLE EBLOG, 2013

NΩ

"... I would recommend to people is that they always take a long-term point of view. I think this is something about which there's a lot of controversy. A lot of people — and I'm just not one of them — believe that you should live for the now. I think what you do is think about the great expanse of time ahead of you and try to make sure that you're planning for that in a way that's going to leave you ultimately satisfied. This is the way it works for me. There are a lot of paths to satisfaction and you need to find one that works for you."
BEZOS, 2008

NΩ

I tend to be myopic. I tend to defer to what is in front of my face — in my immediate proximity in time and space. What's in the fridge — I tend to eat, even too much. What's on the TV — I tend to watch, regardless of the quality. But this tendency to defer to convenience is a formula for underachievement, or even

worse. It requires will to keep my brain focused on the implications of my actions. But such perspective is the origin of the creative, positive action. And no important human accomplishment from the beginning of time came from such myopic perspective. In fact, just the contrary.

The dominance of short-term temporal perspectives causes irresponsibility and suffering. In the 1946 Nuremberg trials, the Nazi leadership deferred to orders from superiors as a way to excuse the atrocities they committed. "I had received Gen. Bader's orders to shoot prisoners ... <but> I did not bear any responsibility. I may have thought about these things only for reasons of humanity. My Commander-in-Chief alone bore the military responsibility. I was only Chief of Staff, and, as such, I was only his assistant." (Tribunal, 1947) Von Geitner's testimony demonstrates that his fear of responsibility prohibited him from seriously considering the implications of the order, much less acting even "... for reasons of humanity".

> *"We all live under the same sky,*
> *but we all don't have the same horizon."*
> ADENAUER, 1972

Konrad Adenaurer was the successful Chancellor of post-war Germany. His famous "horizon" quote underlines the brutal reality that many see much further than me.

Whether I like it or not, I am confronted with a choice of temporal perspective, which I either accept with certainty or decline to circumstance. I've tried no purpose at all, ambling a path and placing one foot before the other with little motive beyond survival. I've tried giving little thought to specific goals, beyond "I want more!" — more stuff for me and making more of my identity. I've tried believing purpose is predestined by God or Nature — a dogma-directed identity, giving little importance to my individual motivation beyond going with the flow. I've tried tangible goals — avoiding, struggling, and overcoming obstacles for a living, hoping someday, maybe, I could rest in peace. I tried these and more, and still I was unsatisfied and riddled with doubt. That is, until a conversation I had in March 2012 with John C. Bogle. I'm sure he couldn't have imagined how his words would haunt me — but they resonated powerfully with the a quote I'd memorized years before.

"We cannot escape history."
LINCOLN, 1862

Imagine for a moment that Lincoln's statement is a true and provable Law of Physics regarding the contribution of each individual to history. That, to a greater or lesser degree, each of my actions — and the actions of those before and contemporary to me — weave irrevocably into the fabric of each manifesting moment. Just as the wave created by each drop of rain falling on the surface of a lake combine to a torrent, so "drops" combine with the multitude of others' actions to create my experience of reality at any given instant. Lincoln's logic is inescapable. I determine the world I experience through my choice of actions. And the lives of the generations to follow will either benefit or be diminished by my choice of action. There is no escaping it.

"This story shall the good man teach his son;
And Crispin Crispian shall ne'er go by,
From this day to the ending of the world,
But we in it shall be remember'd ..."
SHAKESPEARE, 1600

6.1 — Gospel of St. Jack

Likely that Jack Bogle would not remember my name, but I knew something about Jack Bogle. In the Fall 2012, as Chairman of Magellan Leadership, we were considering candidates for our inaugural Intrepid Leader Award (ILA), to recognize leaders who, like Magellan, matched their important achievements with a talent for engendering an almost numinous loyalty among their colleagues and followers.

One candidate for the award was John C. Bogle, founder of the Vanguard Group. Cited by Forbes as one of the top three financial minds of the 20th century, I'd read a few of his books and was verging on becoming a "Boglehead," the term for followers of the financial gospels according to "St. Jack." His life's work enabled millions to accumulate trillions in wealth via innovations in no-load, indexed mutual funds. But Bogle's legendary reputation didn't stand on his business genius and philanthropy alone. A material pauper compared to his peers, he was an iconoclast. And the wisdom contained in his many books, articles, and interviews combined to elevate Jack's reputation to mythical proportions.

He seemed the epitome of the intrepid leader, and I was determined that he would be the first recipient of the ILA. I was fired up with anticipation that my recruiting mission would allow me at least a few minutes conversation with this historic leader. I'd learned that great leaders, like Lincoln, can communicate in a few words what others can't communicate in a thousand. If I had the presence of mind to listen, these words could be life changing, and I was going to be paying close attention to Mr. Bogle.

Following failed attempts to reach him through his publisher, I happened across his blog (Bogle) and began commenting on his postings. Before long we had a dialog going which would eventually lead to a telephone conversation where I pitched my case for his receiving the Intrepid Leader Award. He was reluctant to engage on the topic. He'd been approached by many looking to do an exposé on his leadership of the 75,000-crew strong Vanguard Group.

"I'm not interested in that leadership stuff!" is the way I recall his response. My sense was that he found such self-analysis uninteresting, lacking the intellectual rigor of quantitative inquiry into the miracle of commission-free, compound-investment growth. I'd hit a dead end until reading the scriptural reference posted at the masthead of his blog. Here was a statement of purpose. Perhaps there was a deep and powerful current that had directed the extraordinary voyage of Vanguard.

> *"If the trumpet gives and uncertain sound,*
> *who shall prepare himself for battle?"*
> PAUL

"Uncertain" was a word that had troubled me since fourth semester physics at Cal, and Werner Heisenberg's (Heisenberg W. , 1927) eminent Uncertainty Principle (HUP) was the root of it. HUP basically argued (to my oversimplifying brain), that uncertainty was a condition of the human experience. How could I square HUP with Bogle's biblical tag line that uncertainty presaged defeat? Was his leadership secret explained by his fervor to battle with the fundamentals of uncertainty? I wondered if a key to his success was the certainty he created through his relentless "trumpeting" about the powerful wealth creation that's possible through indexed investing. Bogle came to personify his product, and I reckoned that somehow such monolithic allegiance to his mutual-fund mandate — first espoused as an undergrad at Princeton — was part of what had inspired multitudes to follow St. Jack.

This epiphany moved me from admirer to devotee. Despite his reluctance to speak, I now believed that I'd cracked part of Bogle's Code. I was more determined than ever to see him speaking to the members of Magellan about his other leadership keys. A contrarian and self-described "introvert," venturing much beyond quantitative financial conversations wasn't a priority for him. As I pursued him, I began sensing that he'd wished he'd never responded to my blog comment. But I kept pressing, until, at one point in the course of my "stalking," he admonished me with a six-word response that turned out to be the second and most important certainty key, which I refer to as St. Jack's Law:

> *"Never forget, your horizon is forever."*
> BOGLE, THE BOGLE EBLOG, 2013

On a different, more distracted day this statement might have passed as just another platitude — a sound bite from a writer prone to the poetic. But considering the source, it gave me pause. Why would an individual with such an unparalleled résumé of financial, philanthropic, and literary achievement make such an arcane statement to a leadership stalker? It so happened that at the same time I had been reading Lincoln on Leadership (Williams, 1993), and Bogle's advice reminded me of the quote from the president's 1862 address to congress:

> *"No relative significance or insignificance will spare one or another of us. The fiery trials through which we pass will light us down in honor or dishonor to the latest generation.*
> *We, even we here, hold the power and bear the responsibility."*
> LINCOLN, 1862

Did Mr. Bogle and Mr. Lincoln have a common leadership denominator? Was there something fundamental in holding a mortality exceeding personal perspective that fostered followers? I began digging deep into Bogle's writings, but was unable to come up with another reference. Somewhere deep in the caverns of my learnings on leadership, St. Jack's statement began resonating. My brain began linking his remark to similar soundings of Plato's Allegory of the Cave (Plato, 380 BC), Epictetus' Enchiridion (Epictetus, AD c. 125), Marcus Aurelius' Meditations (Aurelius, AD c. 170), Pascal' Dilemma (Pascal, 1670), Mirandola (Mirandola G. P., 1486), Adenaurer (Adenauer, 1972), Frankl (Frankl, 1946) the Gautama (Gautama, c. 450 BC), and others who had variously referred to the benefits of unlimited perspectives on my place in the world. But, what precisely did he intend by writing it to me? I asked him on his blog. No response. Six months later I had the chance to ask him, in front of the entire Magellan audience, and he tactfully avoided a direct answer. During a face-to-face meeting in his office some weeks later he deflected my direct question about the meaning of the remark, restating his indifference to conversations about ". . . the leadership thing."

Deciphering Mr. Bogle was left to my imagination. Like Magellan's mission to discover a sea course that circled the world, understanding St. Jack's words sent me on an odyssey of discovery. One of the great minds of the 20th century had given me a glimpse of one of his operating principles, and it became my purpose to fathom its meaning. John C. Bogle passed away in early 2019, without revealing to me the secret of "Your horizons are forever." This book is the chronicle of my efforts to decipher "forever horizons" in the context of leadership: problem-solving, decision-making, and action-taking. I call it "The Certainty Principle" because deciphering Mr. Bogle's guidance has brought me clarity and confidence. Any problem to which the axiom is applied is distilled and brought into proper perspective, and, in the process, shifted from the myopia of relativity (the absence of absolute values) to the reality of fundamentals that can only be experienced through the adoption of the very long view.

My findings may or may not bear a resemblance to what Mr. Bogle himself had in mind when he planted this bug in my brain five years ago. He's gone, so I'll never know for certain. That said, I can testify that the guidance it has provided me has been important. It enriches every aspect of my life, reframing true achievement into a context that is in a word, "timeless." This jewel of a directive has faceted into many applications, each one adding to the brilliance of the whole. From leadership to purpose to identity to vision to duty to accountability to courage, etc., it seems that no aspect of human experience is beyond the influence of Mr. Bogle's "forever horizon."

6.2 — "Forevering"

Forevering (def.): seeking to understand and embrace my accurate place, and mandate beyond the domain of my own mortality.

At 11, his death was a turning point in my life. I recall my grandfather Earl Leister as a kind, confident, and courageous Santa Claus. He owned a small precision-casting foundry in North Wales, Pennsylvania. As a small boy, I'd sit a safe distance in a pile of casting sand watching in awe as the great man ladled molten metal from 1,400° crucible into the casting forms. He seemed like a God in his big burn-proof boots, heavy khakis, and leather apron, his face aglow in the light of the furnace. He'd painted a wide yellow circle on the con-

crete around the furnace, and I was warned should never be crossed, especially by a kid. Inside the circle was Pappy's domain, a place of fire and danger, I was told to sit quietly during the pouring process, less he become distracted. One time the molten metal overflowed the form encircling his boot and it immediately burst into flame. He casually kicked the fire out, not missing a step, in the brave ballet of drawing off the liquid aluminum and carefully guiding it into the small ports at the top of the casting forms.

My grandfather's wisdom came to me in his actions and mannerisms, not his admonitions. I don't recall his words well. But my images of him hard at work from dawn until dinner, organizing his tools and his desk, tending his rose garden, or sitting in his rocking chair calmly smoking his pipe while reading the paper are indelible. Doubtless my Norman Rockwell images airbrushes the reality. I know for example, that in the latter half of the 1950s, his business was struggling. My mother claimed that it was the cause that killed him (though my Dad said it was his diet of scrapple and apple pie). But the strength and certainty that pervaded his person, was cast into me as solid as a vein of annealed steel. Despite the challenges of life, I was fortunate to have Pappy as an "anchor to windward."

Pappy's kind confidence stuck with me, elevating me through life, despite my multitude of shortcomings. In turn, I made a point of passing on this sense to my son. During his speech at high school graduation, he spoke of the affirmations I had gleaned from my grandfather's behavior and had constantly reinforced with him. I have no doubt that Pap's influence will carry on in my grandson and his after that, his impact becoming a permanent component of the lineage. Considering the physics of the future, it is clearly impossible for outcomes to evolve otherwise.

6.3 — Long-Term Temporal Perspective (LTTP)

Just as each atom of my body will recycle and reform forever after me, so every act I choose to take integrates itself and is perpetuated in the future. What are the implications of implementing St. Jack's Law (SJL) as a guide to my choices of action?

First an understanding of just how different it is.

"Forever horizon" flies in the face of the classical philosophies of the stoics, like Seneca, who prescribe treating time like a rare commodity — being mindful that death may await around the next corner. My "forever horizon" compels me to see my actions in the context of their permanent impact. Though both philosophies focus the brain on personal responsibility for outcomes, "foreverism" sets my perspective on responsibility as permanent, my behavior a never-ending obligation. In effect, I never escape accountability for my actions.

Brains operate in the instant. With a mechanical lack of operational perspective, my brain tends to default to pain avoidance, bouncing pin-ball-like from one situation to another, minimizing challenges to its status quo state or pleasure-seeking, like the chronic Lottery buyer focusing the next thrill or payoff to distract from their boredom. Long-term temporal awareness is an act of will, a measure of maturity. Boredom results from my failure to establish enough time context, which is why boredom, *per se*, tends to be a malady of the young and immature. Growing up creates memories, requires me to build a temporal framework for my experiences so that I can make the sense of, if I so choose, the trajectory of my progress. This is the "connect the dots" perspective so common among uncommon leaders.

> *"You can't connect the dots looking forward;*
> *you can only connect them looking backwards. So, you have to*
> *trust that the dots will somehow connect in your future."*
> JOBS, 2005

> *"Those who cannot remember the past are*
> *condemned to repeat it."*
> SANTAYANA, 1905

But such a perspective is only available to those who take themselves seriously enough to frame themselves in a historical context — those who know their lives are important to the course of civilization.

Lincoln, King, Alexander, Washington, Gandhi, and countless other important influencers framed their lives in the context of "... the great arc of the moral universe" (Parker T., 1850). Choosing a historic perspective within which I execute the tasks, and deal with problems, provides the advantage of reasoning based on fundamental values, rather than seeking momentary identity gratification.

The "forever horizon" is the cognitive context of the evolved human being. Lacking it, I am imprisoned by my hyper-mortality of outcome dependence and addiction to identity. Achieving it, I free myself to do what I must do, abandoning the siren of identity bias.

6.4 — Proximity and Temporal Perspective
"As size is to distance, so value is to time."
PLATO, 380 BC

The proximity effect — the tendency for the human brain to demote future values — is purely captured in Plato's comparison of time and distance. Decreased proximity diminishes significance. A short-term temporal perspective (STTP) diminishes perceived value in time. Future gains of significant value appear smaller, while present gains of little value appear may appear important (Mischel & al., 1972). Ignoring the power of compound growth with respect to savings and investment is an often-sighted example of this brain effect.

Temporal perspective is the time context within which I reason my course of action. Predominantly short-term temporal perspective means that short-term gratification-based decisions will dominate. When presented with a cookie, I eat it, absent a thought of the consequences, because eating it reinforces a reactive pattern of behavior. Such instant gratification is identity-reinforcing because it figuratively and literally (in the case of too many cookies) makes more of "me" (as the modern pandemic of obesity so clearly demonstrates). Similarly, emotion replaces action when I habitually focus on my immediate feelings as the priority. Rather than seeking an understanding of what my feelings signify (what they are pointing to), I seek the quickest path to gratification. Any gratification will do, and gastric fullness is an easy proxy for filling the void of ignorance. Now, sometimes eating a cookie is nothing more than eating a cookie. I get that! But all patterns of instant gratification tend to reinforce short-term behavior that's centered on feeling support and justifying the emotional story defining my identity. "It's all about me!" I don't need to dig any deeper for root cause and an appropriate course of action. The emotional "me cookie" is enough. Little perspective, no reasoning, accountability optional.

Say I come across a person lying in the street, injured and crying out for help. STTP prevents me from considering the consequences of the person's situation because I am enthralled with my own immediate emotional response and the avoidance of emotional discomfort of a deeper think into what I am experiencing, and the rational actions dictated. This phenomenon is known as "the bystander effect."

"I didn't want to get involved."

Beginning at 3:15 a.m. on the morning of March 13, 1964, Catherine "Kitty" Genovese was raped and murdered by Winston Moseley in an alley behind an apartment building in Queens, N.Y. Police interviews documented that, over the course of the 30-minute attack, 37 people were either watching it happen or could hear Genovese screaming for help. Yet none took action. Minutes after the attack ended a neighbor, Karl Ross, finally called a friend for advice on what to do. That friend then called another friend who finally called the police. Genovese died in an ambulance an hour after the attack had begun. The crime got little attention until a NEW YORK TIMES article (Gansberg, 1964) quoted a witness as stating, "I didn't want to get involved." That triggered public outrage (a group identity phenomenon) about urban apathy, and subsequent studies into what is known as "the "bystander effect" (Darley & Latane, 1968).

Don't be a

$$\frac{d^3 x}{d t^3}$$

Lacking a persistent framework of accountability, STTP promotes a fear response when confronted with the unfamiliar. Since accelerated change is the fundamental of reality, STTP imprisons me in fear and inaction if I allow it to dominate.

STTP is the default state because my brain was born with a reactive amygdala, the center of the fight or flight response. Inherent reactivity tends to subvert the value of decision-making based on the long-term temporal perspectives (LTTP). LTTP dominance establishes a pattern of reasoning on consequences and accountability, but since STTP is the default, LTTP requires cultivation to help it prevail. But how?

6.5 — The Calculus of LTTP

It's tough to break a lifetime habit of short-term thinking. However, becoming skilled early in the disciplines of long-term temporal perspective makes life more manageable and productive. The oath of military service promises to support and defend the Constitution, clearly a LTTP reinforced by months of training and years of practical reinforcement. Is it a coincidence that U.S. veteran households are economically better off than those of non-vets (Bennett, 2019)? I wasn't so disciplined, but as the benefit of LTTP became clear to me, I became interested in learning how to use it. I noticed that those who create enduring value seem to have mastered LTTP.

Though ambition and aspiration are key to achievement, we'd still be living in caves if not for those who learned to develop their LTTP. No airplanes, no batteries, no calculus, no zippers[1]. None came from the myopic masses of short-term thinkers. So, if the long view prevails as the strategy of achievement, what then of the very, very long view? What of St. Jack's "forever" principle? What are the consequences when the domain of reasoning is no longer constrained by the rather arbitrary limitations implicit by my lifetime? As a practical matter, what constitutes my "lifetime" is a highly conditional — only minimally within my control. Brains struggle with creating

---

1 – *The Universal Fastener Company (now Talon, Inc.) was founded by Whitcomb Judson, inventor of pneumatic railway systems and Alexander Graham Bell, an epic LTTP thinker.*

and maintaining timelines of accountability when the duration is so variable. Hence, the many who defer responsibility to the fatalistic philosophy, "If it's meant to be . . ."

It is worthwhile to invoke a little mathematics here to precise my point. In calculus terms, my purpose in life can be characterized by the following definite integral:

$$M = \int_{t_0}^{t} V(t)dt, \text{ where } t=?$$

"M" is my meaning, my **MANDATE**, my individual accountability, my purpose. $V(t)$ is the time-dependent function of the values I constantly employ in my decision-making process to achieve that mandate. The integral of my value function creates no meaning when the upper limit of my accountability is undefined. What if $t=1$ week? 1 month? 1 year? How does my mandate change? It gains definition, but I can't see the whole picture, or the whole potential of my values. The only way to see it all is by setting $t=\infty$. Now I can evaluate the entire area under the value curve, and that result of can be astounding.

This integral either converges to a specific mandate (proper) or it diverges into meaninglessness (improper), depending on the nature of $V(t)$. If the latter (meaninglessness), then it's clearly time to reevaluate $V(t)$, i.e., it's time to ask yourself what exactly it is that you believe in. The famous quote attributed to Steve Jobs,

We're here to put a dent in the universe.
Otherwise why else even be here?
SHEFF, 1985

suggests the power of such a limitless perspective on Jobs's domain of accountability to his values.

That my mandate can only manifest itself when I evaluate what really matters to me in the long view is a somewhat uncanny and unsettling finding. Failing to evaluate my purpose in terms of the "forever" principle prevents the self-knowledge from which the well of certainty is plumbed. Otherwise, I am only guessing at meaning. And guessing is not a long-term strategy for achievement.

And what of the t_0 limit? Again, Mr Jobs:

> *"You can't connect the dots looking forward; you can only connect them looking backwards ... You have to trust in something — your gut, destiny, life, karma, whatever."*
> JOBS, 2005

2000 years before Steve Jobs made this famous declaration at Stanford University, Marcus Aurelius admonished the error in ignoring the importance of t_0:

> *"... there's immense importance in learning from the past."*
> AURELIUS, AD C. 170

The Jobs-Aurelius "past dot connecting," it would appear, is about integrating my values from the beginning, whatever the beginning is for me. For me, seeing into my future meant first reaching back into history.

6.6 — Biochemical Immortality

Apparently, immortality is within our grasp. Ray Kurzweil asks: "Do we have the knowledge and the tools today to live forever?" According to models, the "paradigm-shift rate" (the rate of technical progress) is doubling every decade, and the capability (price performance, capacity, and speed) of specific information technologies is doubling every year. So, Kurzweil's answer to the question is a definitive "Yes!"

"The knowledge exists, if aggressively applied, to slow aging and disease processes to such a degree that you can be in good health and good spirits when the more radical life-extending and life-enhancing technologies become available over the next couple of decades." (Kurzweil & Grossman, MD, 2004)

Researcher Helen Blau and her lab at Stanford have discovered a technique for increasing the length of chromosomal telomeres, the DNA "fuse," so to speak, on the cellular aging process.

"Treated cells behave as if they are younger than untreated cells, multiplying with abandon in the laboratory dish rather than stagnating or dying." (Blau, 2015)

Mapping such technology from the petri dish to people will be complicated. But when and how it happens is secondary to the potential impact of radical life extension. After all, does the knowledge that my investments will create enough wealth for my children and grandchildren impact my thinking about finance? The answer is a resounding yes. So, what is the impact of knowing that technology will soon exist with the potential to allow those same grandchildren to live 150+ years?

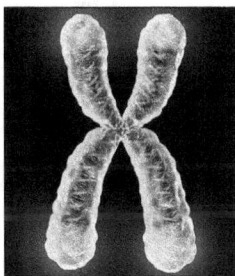

Whether or not I am conscious of it, the mental model of how I perceive myself existentially — as a being — determines the way I interact with myself, with others, and with the world around me. With greater or lesser confidence, I hold an image of my place in the world that serves as a practical template for living, defining my individual identity and the scope or horizon within which that identity functions.

Come with me on a journey to explore the implications of the "death-free-life" that will soon be within reach. Consider what happens when we can replace the old saw, "Nothing's for certain but death and taxes" with "Nothing's for certain but taxes." It may appear at first that this problem is not my problem. But bear with me. What I've discovered is that the practical lessons of a "forever" framework address some of the central challenges that badger us in our mundane lives. NΩ

CHAPTER 7
M IS FOR MANDATE:
—— MANIFEST MY MANDATE ——

Imagine choosing ultimate accountability for actions manifesting the results of my talents and skills for this instant, and for the consequences of my actions forever. What is the value of such a choice, and what is its application? The power resides in the question, "How do my choices change if I frame each one in the context of forever horizons?"

My **MANDATE** is my individual role and responsibility in manifesting the reality around me. My role exists whether or not I decide to seek it out. Finding it and embracing is the central challenge in life. The penalty life exacts for indecision and inattention is despair.

> *"The mass of men lead lives of*
> *quiet desperation."*
> THOREAU, 1854

The Three Stonecutters

On a foggy autumn day in 1201 a lone traveler happened upon a large group of workers at the construction of Salisbury cathedral, adjacent to the River Avon. Despite being

tardy for an important rendezvous, curiosity convinced the traveler that he should inquire about their work. With a slight detour he moved toward the first of the three tradesmen and said, "My dear fellow, what is it that you are doing?" The man continued his work and grumbled, "I am cutting stones." Realizing that the mason did not wish to engage in conversation, the traveler moved toward the second of the three, and repeated the question. To the traveler's delight this man stopped his work, ever so briefly, and stated that he was a stonecutter. He then added, "I came to Salisbury from the north to work, but as soon as I earn ten quid, I will return home." The traveler thanked the second mason, wished him a safe journey home. He headed toward the third of the trio.

When he reached the third worker, he once again asked his original question. This time the worker paused, glanced at the traveler until they made eye contact, and then looked skyward, drawing the traveler's eyes upward. The third mason replied, "I am a mason, and I am building a cathedral." He continued, "I have journeyed many miles to be part of the team that is constructing this magnificent cathedral. I have spent many months away from my family, and I miss them dearly. However, I know how important Salisbury Cathedral will be one day, and I know how many people will find sanctuary and solace here. I know this because the Bishop once told me his vision for this great place. He described how people would come from all parts to worship here. He also told me that the Cathedral would not be completed in our days, but that the future depends on our hard work." He paused and then said, "So I am prepared to be away from my family because I know it is the right thing to do. I hope that one day my son will continue in my footsteps and perhaps even his son if need be."

CALLAHAN, 2008

"Cutting stones," "I earn ten quid," "Constructing this magnificent cathedral." What distinguishes these three masons? I suggest it is perspective. The first man has none. His view is

so narrowed to the task at hand, that he reacts gruffly to being bothered with the traveler's interest in him. Similarly, the
second man focuses on getting paid and escaping the drudg-
ery. The third mason is different — " . . . the Cathedral would
not be completed in our days, but that the future depends on
our hard work." A stone mason works differently when he has
the blueprint, and is skilled in how to use it. But true mastery
happens when the design in mind reaches beyond the page to
the purpose of the work.

As with the medieval masons building the cathedral, my la-
bor is my duty. But mastery of that duty is driven by an understanding of my work's larger significance. Such mastery
gives work meaning. A president's job is leadership, but it is
the meaning behind the work that separates the true leaders
from people managers. Likewise, a carpenter's mandate is
the mastery of his skills, tools, and materials in the domain
of those who will be served by the product of his excellent
work — even if they never know his name. It is an existential
physical irony that though it is impossible for a single human
identity to have any lasting importance in the world (consider
Shelly's "Ozymandus"), their work forever changes each subsequent instant forever.

While individual mandates are unique, mandate classes are
enduring. There will always be farmers, doctors, and software
developers. Individual mandates show up early and are nurtured, neglected, or thwarted. Mandate is a matter of talent,
skill, focus, and circumstance, but mostly native talent and
focus. Mastery manifests naturally, but only if one chooses to
focus and avoid the distractions of conformity to the miserable mean. Like the third mason, to have a mandate means
uncovering that personal horizon that exceeds temporal constraints — the "forever horizon."

The Mandated Individual is compelled first by talent and intuition, and in time by experience and skill, followed then by the courage to discover and rediscover the optimal path of action to supreme mastery. In contrast, the mandate-free Spectator has no such compass, seeking identity by association with outcomes beyond individual control.

Civilization is the story of the distribution of human beings between these two extremes. Mandators make outcome-free choices based on necessities dictated by their horizons. Spectators want to follow others, watching what happens and "going with the flow." They embrace the outcome-based decision-making philosophy.

Because outcomes are uncontrollable under the best of circumstances, outcome-based decision-making leads to the "whipsaw" life. An example: The "buy high-sell low" phenomenon in commodities trading. Most investors are momentum buyers — they commit like lemmings. The Mandator is the opposite of the Spectator in this regard. The Mandator needs to be going the other way, against the crowd. But his motive is not identity-bound. Appearing "cool" is not important. It is defensive action to avoid poisoning the power that made them productive to begin with — protection of their individual mandate. This partially explains Bob Dylan's refusal to attend the Nobel ceremony (Contrera, 2016). Celebrity poisons both the fan and the celebrity. The vanity it promotes distracts from the focus on mandate required to produce works of such exceptional caliber.

The fascination we have with observing animals in the wild explains our natural attraction to Mandators. The behavior of a Mandator resonates as deeply authentic, if not unsettling, and even terrifying. Animals behave instinctively. That authenticity aesthetic is as primordial as sexual arousal (Salu, 2013), originating from the deep instinctive certainty of self-preservation.

Meticulous attention to one's mandate is an antidote to the cycle of fear, regret, and desperation that plagues the uncertain brain. Whether a carpenter or a king, tenacity is the vital discipline of mandate fulfillment. As such, submission to fear and regret is the acid-test of the mandated life.

7.1 — Wrong Choices

> *"The fool who persists in his folly will become wise."*
> BLAKE, 1793

Making a wrong choice of a mandate is not the bad choice. The "bad" choice is no choice at all. Failure can be defined as deferring my mandate to circumstance.

Undaunted by his struggle to fund circumnavigation in his homeland, Magellan (a Portuguese citizen) did the unthinkable in the 15th century Iberia. He went to the King of Spain who promptly said, "Yes!" Doubtless he anticipated the possibility of mutiny, alongside the likelihood of navigating some of the most dangerous waters in the world. But none of this stopped the Captain from pressing on. His mandate of circumnavigation was supreme and infectious, empowering the expedition to overcome devastating setbacks, including the death of Magellan himself late in the voyage. After completing the 42,000-mile route in 609 days, only one of the five ships remained, and only a tenth of the original crew. In a chronicle of the voyage, one of the survivors wrote of Magellan:

> *"… he was our mirror, our light, our comfort,*
> *and our true guide."*
> PIGAFETTA, 1525

Until I commit, it is always easier to succumb to circumstance than to maintain focus on my mandate. Certainty means my mandate reigns supreme, regardless of circumstance, regardless of outcomes, for all time.

7.2 — The Frankl Mandate

"Life ultimately means taking the responsibility to find the right answer to its problems and to fulfill the tasks which it constantly sets for each individual."
FRANKL, 1946

Frankl's mandate is a simple, yet powerful, directive that fixes confusion and promotes determination. He tells me to make a habit of attending to the duties right under my nose. Chuck Yeager echoed this when asked about the perils of being a test pilot.

"Your duty is paramount. You don't say 'I'm not going to do that — that's dangerous. If it's your duty to do it, that's the way it is."
YEAGER, ACHIEVEMENT, 1991

The brain is inclined to rationalize duties. Repetitive avoidance of duty can easily become a chronic state. Identity-seeking is the brain's solution for escaping Frankl's imperative, of escaping responsibly. The cognitive escape from the cascade of challenges I confront inflates my identity, making me right for my wrong choices. I can make myself a victim of my problems and avoid them, or I can identify myself as too important to deal with my problems and seek input that justifies either position.

Powerful identities often flip-flop from one to the other to escape the truth. Bill Cosby drugged his female victims for sex believing that as "America's Dad" he was above accountability for his actions. He denied the charges for years, but when he was indicted, he flipped to the victim persona by claiming blindness and stating he was unable to adequately defend himself if he couldn't see his accusers. Although he was eventually convicted, his "victimhood" delayed justice, triggering a mistrial. Even such a towering talent and mandate as his became corrupted by identity.

7.2.1 — Optimizing Mandate

Optimal human performance is measured by the portion and persistence of my work done in service (my mandate) to my core talent. To the extent that I vary from this mandate, my performance diminishes. I become frustrated. To the extent that I shirk my duty I create waste, uncertainty, or worse. Certainty is created when my horizon is projected from the vantage point of my archetypal talent. Archetypal talent is in my DNA. I am born with it. The great game is identifying it as early as possible, then remaining focused on adding the skills and experience that perfect the native talent. In the Hindu religion, four primordial talent classes are:

- Teachers & Inventors (Brahmins): priests, scholars, and teachers.

- Leaders & Commanders (Kshatriyas): rulers, warriors, and administrators.

- Merchants & Logisticians (Vaishyas): agriculturalists and traders.

- Makers & Enablers (Shudras): laborers and service providers.

Each of these classes are equally important. Social order collapses if one or another is missing. Below each of the four are multiple sub-levels, eventually branching into specialties of individual talent and skill for which a given role is responsible. Certainty grows when the talent for which one is accountable is identified, and attention is focused on, adding the appropriate skills and experience to improve outcomes. Some people are naturally multi-talented. But even for them, transforming oneself from one mandate to another is difficult without significant effort and frustration.

Successfully transforming myself to a mandate that excludes my native talent is impossible. Talent, if discovered early and nurtured, leads to extraordinary achievement. Michelangelo Buonarroti's father owned a marble quarry. After his mother's death at the age of six, Michelangelo went to live near the quarry in the home of his nanny, whose husband happened to be a stone cutter. Hence began his love affair with marble, with magnificent results. Many children with parents working in the marble works grew up in the same town. Yet he was born with a deep intuitive talent for cutting stone, and generations have marveled at the product of his early choice to relinquish all other studies to become a master.

> *"Along with the milk of my nurse, I received the knack of handling chisel and hammer, with which I make my figures."*
> MICHELANGELO

So, what is my talent? A simple question for a child to answer — fireman, doctor, president. But once the brain has had decades to assemble an identity, the question becomes complicated. Becoming an adult, particularly in the digital age, it is easy to misalign with the talent that came "Along with the milk of my nurse . . ." Difficulty in learning new skills, combined with social pressures to conform, can cause me to be swept away by the river of glittering possibilities, which constantly distract — an easy path to popular success, as externally defined. Popular is then the comfortable path. It forgoes the struggle of discovering and manifesting my mandate.

There is pain and suffering in acquiring the skills to master my talents. But the discomfort of such diligence pales in comparison to the consequences of negligence that haunts for a lifetime, and leads, inevitably, to bitterness and regret.

If my horizon is my ideal, then my mandate is my compass. My horizon lies before and behind me. The horizon before me is as great as the ideal extrapolation of my talent mastery can take me. The horizon behind me is formed by the series of achievements that originate at the source of my talent at its vanishing point. I form the line by linking a series of definitive "way points" in the past. A candid examination of these way points creates a line pointing in one direction. The origin of that line is my archetypal talent. Once I begin seeing my mission — my duty as the fulfillment of the application of my talent — my horizon expands to accommodate the possibilities. This is the principle reason that money (for its own sake) fails as a prime human motivation. Money is not a talent in search of fulfillment. It can, at best, be an abstraction for my level of mastery, if indeed money is an adequate measure for my given talent. But not all talents can be evaluated in currency. Such talents will cause terrific frustration for me if I insist on trying to evaluate them in terms of revenue generated.

7.3 — Asking

The question that clarifies mandate is the same question asked at any stage in life. What are the important experiences, activities, or accomplishments — perhaps even unsolicited complements or recognitions — pointing to? Before the age of 5? By the age of 10? 12?, 17?, etc. Which experiences are unique, as opposed to mundane and commonplace? I can make a list of these and plumb my memory for details related to what made them particularly memorable. These reality-testing questions help clarify my mandate:

- Is it accurate (True or False)?

- What pictures come to mind when you recall the experience?

- How precisely can you describe the experience?

- How significant was the experience to your future decisions?

- How relevant was the experience to what came before or after?

- Was the experience logical at the time? Did it fit in a logical sequence with other experiences?

- What was the breadth of the experience? Did it have a narrow or broad impact on subsequent events?

Once this exercise is complete, try connecting the dots between those experiences that have the greatest impact, seeking to identify the common thread.

7.4 — Horizon and Mandate

My process of deciphering Bogle's forever horizon was like coming home. The conclusion that there is no escaping accountability for my choices of action is like arriving back where it all started — childlike clarity between right and wrong, true and false. Myopic judgment is bounded by peer pressure, politics, and the vanity of identity. Capitulation to the unlimited accountability for my choices is comforting because it is so fundamentally and irrefutably certain, relieving me of years of artificial identity constraints. My brain differentiates for a living. That's what I "pay" it for. But such calculus diminishes me when the brain's problem-solving processes venture too far from the wisdom that great perspectives provide.

Choosing expedience over perspective I venture farther and farther from wisdom. Short horizons bring waywardness, leading to confusion, boredom, and fear. I understood that acquiring wisdom matters. Once I accepted that, like it or not, there was no escaping the physics of the consequences of my actions. A fix on forever assures that my choices of action will be wisely aligned with values of my life's **MANDATE**.

CEOs lead, senators cast votes, doctors diagnose, all based on their self-interests, but those interests change based on their perspective on their individual accountability. Aligning brain work with a horizon sets up a self-reinforcing cycle. The longer my horizon, the more numerous the "stars" there are in alignment and the more important the picture my mandate becomes to my work. For better or worse, those who change history perceive themselves historically.

> *"We cannot escape history ... no relative significance or insignificance will spare one or another of us."*
> LINCOLN, 1862

7.5 — Mandate Tenacity
The struggle to master a mandate is tedious, tiring, even dangerous work. Learning to hike high terrain is tough, the legs

burn as the muscles build. Climbing back down is a little easier, requiring only the skill and confidence to avoid falling. But there's always a higher hill to climb out on the horizon, so long as one maintains the confidence and focus to climb it.

"Those that reach their goals perish."
REINHOLD MESSNER

My forward momentum is maintained as long as unlimited possibility is my central operating perspective. Again, like alternatively hiking up and down an elevation, I must pay attention to the path. Distractions are, well, distracting! Periodically checking my progress against my horizon keeps me on route. Daily reminders of where I'm headed enable me to keep the struggle in perspective.

My last thought at night and my first thought in the morning is TCP. "My horizon is forever" is no longer an abstraction. It is a device for keeping the impingements of the external world at bay. Sailing ships have a ballast keel enabling them to remain upright against the force of wind. When the boat is tacking and jibing, the keel counters the torque produced by the wind on the sail. TCP is the ballast keel that enables me to make the necessary course adjustments that would be fearful, or even impossible, without it. Establishing my busines with confidence is enabled by knowing that doing so is a necessity of my mandate. TCP dictates that I have no other choice, regardless of the apparent impediments.

Whether or not "Bogle's Bombshell" was intended to convey all this is immaterial at this point. His words felt primal, as if I'd been given one of the great keys to it all. It's important to mention here that "foreverism" was not in any sense a religious revelation for me. It was like finally finding the bedrock after a long dig. It was like putting my hands on something solid, durable, and practical — of being grounded. The same truth that has been communicated to me through the wisdom of great thinkers, remained unacknowledged until I received that message. And I never looked back.

This is not to say that such a revelation was encouraging. The prospect that there is way out of absolute accountability was, at first, nauseating. I wondered: Did "foreverism" imply that I was destined to be the victim of the situations I encountered? Was I a rudderless boat bobbing on a great ocean of conditionals without a map? Or did it mean learning to fashion a rudder and sextant, navigate the course to my goals, and adapt and correct for conditions as I encountered them?

Liberation came from this surrender to self-reliance. Discovering permanent self-accountability meant eliminating reliance on forces beyond my control that influence my outcomes while committing deeply to those within my control. What I call my incomes. My duty was to deal with the unique tasks and problems encountered with the incomes within my control. A deeper understanding came to me: It does not matter whether there was a way out of my accountability or not. Foreverism is a decision. It is its own reward. It is far more exciting for me to assume ultimate and eternal responsibility for this instant than any alternative frame of reference I could choose to adopt.

In this sense the Certainty Principle is a bit like climate change. The science is a little foggy, but in some final analysis it may be a better choice to err on the side of residual personal accountability. In TCP we tackle as scientifically as possible this question: What is the value of knowing I am forever? What are the implications to purpose, outcomes, and my identity? NΩ

CHAPTER 8
IN IS FOR INCOMES:
—— ACCOUNT MY INCOMES ——

"Compound interest is the 8th wonder of the world.
He who understands it earns it, he who doesn't, pays it."
ATTRIBUTED TO A. EINSTEIN

Incomes are monies, value, or benefit received in exchange for work or investment. Certainty requires calculating and keeping track — a numerical accounting of value, both prospective and returned, from my decisions and actions. Achieving any mandate is impossible without keeping account.

"The general who wins a battle
makes many calculations in
his temple (brain) before the
battle is fought. The general
who loses a battle makes but
few calculations."
TZU S. , 5TH CENTURY BC

Living is not war, of course, but war is a rather unforgiving form of living. Manifesting mandates requires vigilance preventing me from drifting into unsubstantiated reasoning that could, in Sun Tzu's example, literally kill me. Focus needs numbers because the brain, as with the paramecium, is, at its root, a counting device. When I account and communicate numerically, I am speaking the least ambiguous language of neurologics. Therefore, Sun Tzu's advice generalizes to the achievement of any mandate: What I can count, I can conquer. An identity-focus causes me to drift. But scoring brings me back to the reality track.

Once, while going through a particularly trying family episode, I decided to build a deck on my house. The project was tedious at times, but refining my technique for measuring cuts and angles calmed me down. There was immense pleasure in learning to calculate a perfect fit.

There is wonder in numbers. But what numbers really matter? Not all numbers that appear relevant are relevant to achievement of my mandate. For years I believed that revenue dollars were the key measure of my success, until I discovered that these dollars were only a byproduct of my activities. A high activity level delivered higher dollars. Some successful companies have learned to excel by focusing on numbers other than top and bottom line, knowing that revenues come by tuning into the fundamentals that drive them.

"Focus on cost improvement makes it possible for us to afford lower prices, which drives growth. Growth spreads fixed costs across more sales, reducing cost per unit, which makes possible more price reductions. Customers like this, and it's good for shareholders. Please expect us to repeat this loop."
JEFF BEZOS

8.1 — Why "Scoring Is Boring"

Boredom is a vanity disease, born from a habit of ignoring objective reality. I avoid confronting facts because of the identity discomfort when objective measures run contrary to my beliefs and commitments. Am I more inclined to check my account balances when they are growing, or when they are

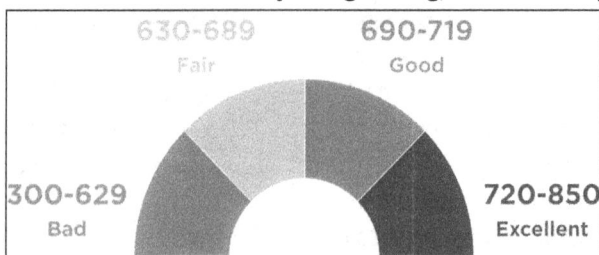

shrinking or in the red? When I lose, do I reject the loss as illegitimate? (See "identity politics" below.) Avoiding objective measure is a special case of confirmation bias — the tendency to ignore or distort data in defense of my preconceptions to preserve my identity.

> *"When men wish to support a theory,*
> *how they torture facts into their service!"*
> MACKAY, 1841

I'm happy to be measured, so long as the numbers support my expectations. But when my numbers look bad, I may be reluctant to heed them to preserve my sense of pride. Leadership that is afflicted with this face-saving phobia can spiral into a dangerous culture of reality avoidance. TCP teaches us to depose identity for just this reason. The courage to confront reality is what remains once I've abandoned vanity of self. In effect, there is never any good or bad data, except that my identity makes it so. There is only data. There is only reality. Ignoring that fact can have unfortunate, even catastrophic, effects.

Face-Saving Haste: The Challenger Disaster

The decision of the engineers at Morton Thiokol to delay the launch of the Challenger was vetoed by management at NASA. The numbers were bad. Ambient temperature at the Cape was far below the 40-degree minimum operating specification for the O-rings on their rocket boosters. Having personally committed to the U.S. Congress on the high-profile launch (schoolteacher

Christa McAuliffe was aboard), management's impatience overruled the numbers. Sadly, the numbers prevailed (Silverman, 2020). Was it the cold or conceit that caused the disaster?

Arrogance at Agincourt

Though the French outnumbered the English at least 4:1, the October 1415 Battle of Agincourt was an English victory with a 15:1 casualty ratio. The crushing defeat has been attributed to the English defensive strategy. Archers (two thirds of the English force) were highly skilled at rapid, long-distance shooting. Commander of the French, Boucicaut knew of the numerical superiority of English fire power. But an insulting rebuke by England's King Henry inflamed his arrogance, triggering him to abandon his initial plan to flank. Instead, he launched a frontal calvary charge. The English showered the advancing French soldiers with 1,000 arrows per second from a fortified position, throwing the French horsemen into chaos.[2] Arrow quills were "thick as snow" (History Magazine, 1999), rendering the French numerical advantage meaningless. Was it the arrows or vanity that slew the French? NΩ

---

2 – The French did not at first credit the major victories of the English to the longbow, but to other tactics, especially the use of the English knights fighting on foot. The French did start to train some infantry in the use of the longbow in the late 1300s, but the king was most concerned about peasants having such powerful weapons. The idea was dropped.

CHAPTER 9
O IS FOR OUTCOMES:
— SURRENDER MY OUTCOMES —

"You really don't think about the outcome ... because you really have no control over it. You concentrate on what you are doing to do the best job you can ..."
YEAGER, ACHIEVEMENT, 1991

When Chuck Yeager beat the sound barrier in October 1947, he was focusing on doing his job, not the outcome. Such important, even dangerous, achievements take courage and focus, because there's little room for outcome obsession out there on the razor's edge of the possible.

"... up there (on the mountain) we want to find long, hard days — days when we don't know in the morning what the evening will bring. It's time we ... searched again for the limits of possibility, for we must have such limits if we are going to use the virtue of courage to approach them. Where else will be able to find refuge in our flight from the oppression of everyday humdrum routine?"
MESSNER, 1971

Reinhold Messner, the most accomplished alpinist of all time, is consumed by his courage to confront the impossible. Certainty is courageous confidence, which decreases with my vigilance of my addiction to outcomes over actions.

To achieve, I must separate the control of my decision-making from the conditional, and, therefore, uncertain outcomes they invariably produce. "I am the ship, not the wake" is a good metaphor for this awareness. Plans dictated by goals are as necessary as a compass, but outcomes (the wake) are not my actions (the ship). They are physically different.

To the extent that I am enthralled with outcomes, I will consistently fail. To the extent that I am enthralled with my deliberate path-finding actions, achievement is assured because control of my actions is absolute.

The bearing of a ship is a measure of the ideal compass direction with respect to a distant target. However, course corrections are always required along the way, as warranted by weather and currents. On occasion, this can mean changing the target itself, as conditions either prevent reaching the destination, or indicate a more favorable destination. Similarly, goals and objectives require learning along the way that inform next action steps. If a step fails, back up and try a different action step. If I make the outcome of each step on the path my priority, I'm bound for disappointment because there are myriad unforeseen obstacles intermediate to goal getting.

Certainty is doing what I must do, independent of outcome. Optimally, I am the "doing," not the "done." I am a verb, not a noun. Therefore, I am only limited by my enthrallment with the expected or resulting outcomes of my actions.

Identity through outcomes is the brain seeking emotional gratification through the way things happen to turn out. The trouble is, the outcome of each one of my actions, in some degree or another, is subject to conditions beyond my control. I am aware of Messrs. Yeager and Messner because of their extraordinary achievements, i.e., the great outcomes they delivered after years of hard work. But I typically give little thought to the myriad poor outcomes they encountered along the path to their achievements. Setbacks didn't stop them because their commitment to "doing the best job" was paramount. The outcome was just the data that proved or disproved a particular approach or technique. Their success resulted from focusing on the quality of their work and ignoring the outcomes, except for the data it provided.

Certainty comes in the degree to which I learn to detached myself from the outcome of my actions. This is not the same as acting without considering the probable outcomes. That's irresponsibility. It is deliberate taking of an action without attaching oneself to the result, because the result is a combination of my decision and conditions, those independent variables beyond my control.

I maintain my car so it will take me where I want to go, safely and without a breakdown. But a random nail in the road can still result in a flat tire, even though I did my best to avoid such a failure. But how many times have I allowed my self-confidence to be broken by circumstances beyond my control?

A dear friend of mine developed brain cancer. It so happens that I know a few medical professionals in that field, so I decided to make it my personal goal to identify the best programs for treating his specific type of cancer, and to help him to assess and access the treatments. I investigated the options and helped him develop a plan of action. What I failed to seriously consider at the time was that the outcomes for brain cancer are statistically grim. Enlisting myself in the effort, my identification with a positive outcome became so compelling, that when he finally succumbed to the disease I was shaken to the point of denial. My goal had been fixed on a cure for his cancer, rather than the more vital one of demonstrating my love and loyalty. To this day, nearly a year later, I still find it difficult to accept that he died after my enthrallment with curing him. This story exposes a rather obvious failure of reasoning on my part: A systematic vulnerability based on hope over reason. It also reveals the powerful forces at work in my brain that instinctively seek identification with unreasonably biased outcomes.

While the brain's identification with outcomes delivers disappointment to its victims, it can be monetized by those who have learned to exploit the vulnerability.

9.1 — Exploiting Hope & Despair: Spectatorship, Media, and Religion

More mundane examples of my brain seeking acknowledgment by attaching to outcomes are unrelenting. Celebrities purposefully leverage the public's fascination with the events in their lives, knowing it's a foolish distraction that delivers them dollars. Religion leverages the notion of original sin (past outcomes) and the promise of redemption and heaven (future outcomes) to enlist followers and command their support. I go to a football game enthralled with the success of "my team," regardless of the odds to escape my own laziness and lack of initiative. I watch popular TV news, mesmerized by the tragic outcomes of others, in an effort to mitigate the guilt for my own lack of achievement.

Enthrallment with outcomes perpetuates the spectator brain-set. Spectatorship replaces focus on what I directly control with the indirect and conditional hope and despair of others. The business of spectatorship and viewership exploits this brain vulnerability. Regardless of the venue, "spectator events" of all kinds leverage my brain's emotional enthrallment with outcomes beyond my control. Despite the reality that my observation has little impact on the outcome of a football match, my emotional enthrallment is compelling, even if I'm only watching it on TV! As a spectator, my identity investment in outcomes is its own reward. Win, lose, or draw, my identity is enhanced through attachment to the outcomes of million-dollar players. In a sense, I am paying a price to accept the experience of loss because an abstract loss is an experience that prevents me from fully confronting my own failures. After all, if the Eagles can lose, how bad can it be when I screw up. To be certain, I must, over and over, confront failure and fix it. I must want to win, and be willing to passionately fight through hell and high water to win, for my own account. This is much different than having a passion for the "Fighting Eagles."

Spectatorship is a harmlessly entertaining, even symbiotic, delusion, as long as I'm aware of the delusion. Unaware, spectatorship becomes a thin proxy for real life. I defer the desperation of my inaction by experiencing vicariously the actions of others. Philadelphia Eagles owner Jeffery Lurie watches every game, but he is not a spectator. Such "makers and creators" understand that the opiate of spectatorship makes them lots of money. Conversely, being a devoted fan emasculates individual accountability, an outcome for which millions willingly pay billions.

Emperor Nero knew how to emasculate the citizenry. In 64 AD nearly 70 percent of Rome burned to the ground. Accusations that Nero's megalomania was to blame for the fire triggered a vicious back lash by the Emperor. He foiled his opponents with a propaganda campaign, attributing the disaster the rabble-rousing Christians, then initiating the brutal spectacle of public persecution in the Colosseum. His plan worked! The people of Rome were sufficiently placated by the sadistic amusements that the tyrant remained in power an additional four years before finally killing himself. Why was the revolt against him quelled by such a ruthless display of power? Why were regular public spectacles of torture perpetuated as a device of political control for the next 200 years?

Hooliganism — violent and disorderly behavior spawned at or after sporting events — is a well-studied aspect of spectatorship. Sports studies scholars Paul Gow and Joel Rookwood at Liverpool-Hope University found in a 2008 study that:

"Involvement in football violence can be explained in relation to a number of factors relating to interaction, identity, legitimacy, and power. Football violence is also thought to reflect expressions of strong emotional ties to a football team, which may help to reinforce a supporter's sense of identity."
GOW & ROOKWOOD, (2008)

Intense identification with external events can permit an individual, albeit temporarily, to abandon the internal accountability that anchors their behavior to reality. The brain of the pathological spectator is fundamentally hijacked by the promise of a synthetic spike in identity (via dopamine, oxytocin, and serotonin) through association with the celebrity of the overall event. Hence, professional sports are often characterized as a "religion" in popular media, with all the trappings. Chants, songs, and logo-ed clothing all help perpetuate the effect of an identity boost through external association.

But when my team fails, my identity fails also. Such are the pitfalls of identification with externals. Spectators' focus on outcomes represents the brain's addiction to identity wherever it can be found, even if it needs to be bought or borrowed from another for the price of an admission ticket. Just observe the post-game faces of fans of a losing team compared to the faces of the players. The fans are often crest-fallen, depressed, even violent. The players sadly march back to the locker room only to smile as they collect the millions the fans are paying them for the vicarious emotional roller coaster called spectatorship.

Spare me the time, efforts, and money! My individual ideas, challenges, decisions, and performance are paramount. And optimizing them requires resources. The courage and tenacity to act on my individual mandate will prove to be exciting enough! TCP shows how my deference to distractions limits my achievements. To win at my mandate, the behaviors of others, regardless of their celebrity, must be rendered for whatever valuable data it holds. Further, those behaviors must be ignored as mere background noise. I become my own spectator, being careful to remain aligned with my priorities — focused on the quality and character of my actions.

9.2 — Identity Politics And Propaganda

Politicization of identity is the central purpose of the propaganda of many political movements. Hillary Clinton's "I'm With Her" (therefore I'm special) campaign slogan leveraged individual-identity-addiction — the hapless desire to seek personal meaning in powerful external associations. When the outcome is (as it always is) disappointing, the results can be devastating, even to denial of reality, or worse. Religious teachings are filled with gruesome stories about the

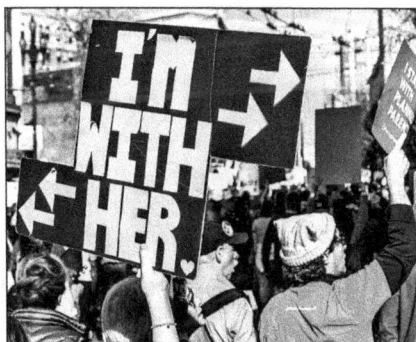

consequences of vanity politics, not the least of which is the story of Jesus. He constantly taught the dangers of self-righteousness:

> *"… all who exalt themselves will be humbled, and those who humble themselves will be exalted."*
> BIBLE, 1611

Still his followers mainly turned on him in the frenzy of the Roman prosecution. The governor Pontius Pilate surrendered the fate of Jesus to the crowd of followers, but it was the righteousness of the crowd that crucified him.

After failing to lead them to victory, the humiliating loss of face drove the Italian people to turn on Mussolini, executing him in the streets. They kicked and spat on his body before hanging it upside down from the roof of a gas station and stoning it.

9.3 — Identity Marketing

Media marketing that leverages my identity's powerful attachments is predictably effective, no matter how outrageous the messaging. My disappointment that attractive women do not flock to my table when I am drinking Dos Equis® beer does little to stem the appeal of "The Most Interesting Man In The World" advertising to my identity. Who knows, maybe I just had an off night. Truth is, I've deferred my beer preference to the marketing. Who cares what it tastes like. Product quality is secondary when my identity is the real product, begging the question: When I choose to buy a product, what am I really buying?

9.4 — Control And Condition

"The difference between successful people and really successful people is that really successful people say no to almost everything."
BUFFETT, 2018

The scope of my personal mandate is defined by my personal domain of control. One might say that as my mandate is "predestined" by the confluence of my DNA, my ambition, and my consequence, so is my domain control likewise prescribed. But to streamline the mission, let's remove consequence. Reliance on circumstance anchors down achievement.

Thus, my achievements are my "Mandate DNA" plus my determination to fulfill my mandate. That creates a domain of decisions and actions for which — and this is the tough part — TCP requires that I swear to control with the devotion of a zealot. My domain of control is circumscribed by the set of actions required in service to my mandate.

TCP suggests that I am meticulous about my mandate. I'm always digging like a hungry dog to get to the fundamentals of cause and effect that elevate the level of my performance. This requirement disambiguates life. My choices of action are constrained to those that are directly impactful within my domain of accountability, which I pursue with as much of my energies as I can muster. All other choices are conditional and do not deserve the expenditure of reasoning, emotion, and energy that define my capacity to do my work superbly.

> *"Laymen know the tricks and techniques. Masters dig deeper into understanding the keys of great work, while knowing that learning alone isn't enough. They've gotten into the habit of practicing — the repetition needed for figuring out exactly where and how each key fits until it becomes automatic."*
> LIGHT, 2019

Conditionals are domains of influence that fall beyond the perimeter of my mandate. There are two types.

1. Not-My Conditionals: These have no impact on my work, and should be categorically ignored. These "not-my-business" influences are like pop-up ads on a cell phone — distractions that can distort and sap attention if my brain allows them to.

2. Obstacle Conditionals: These directly impinge on my actions, and should be adapted to or eliminated. Rain is an obstacle. If it impedes my progress, I respond by raising an umbrella or I get wet.

I ignore the first type altogether because such distractions drain the essential vitality required to fulfill my mandatory responsibilities. TV, social media, judgementalism, and other vanity-based preoccupations must be shunned if I am to succeed spectacularly at my mandate.

But occasionally conditions confront and confound my progress. Rapid response in handling them prevents them from evolving into important obstacles to my goals.

There is a great sense of relief associated with abandoning attachment to identity. I am no longer tethered to the anchor of feeling a cause or effect for everything in the environment. I

am with cause, with effect. I can identify the domain boundaries within which I have greater control, and the larger domains within which condition is in control. My domain of absolute control is much smaller than my identity leads me to believe. Those mandate-predicated decisions and actions that I take on an ongoing basis, independent of outcomes, is the tiny domain for which I am personally responsible. Therefore, the importance of focusing on very few objectives at any given time, and concentrating diligently on detecting and solving problems within that domain, are key to certainty.

Though I carefully choose the clothes I wear — the shirt, the jacket, the pants, the shoes, and even the umbrella I carry — I have no influence over the weather when I walk out the door. Therefore, my choice of clothing is important, because it is of my own choosing, based on my own decisions, my own needs and wants, and my own proclivities. Therefore, even relinquishing the way I dress to the fashion of others (conforming), is an important and dangerous precedent. So make such choices carefully. I surrender no liberties within my domain without a fight, and then still I never, never, ever give in.

Base your actions on the values that are authentic to you. They are deep and driven by the mandate and the horizon you've created for yourself.

In this context, it is easy to understand how Patrick Henry declared, "Give me Liberty, or give me Death." The entire value of human existence comes down to this one point of the liberty and freedom of choice of activity in alignment, and in accordance with, the values that are deeply held by each individual.

It is because those rights, freedoms, and liberties maintain their integrity and are never surrendered that most of human existence is conditional, and that this concept is subject to environmental and situational forces beyond the control of individuals. The great fall of man is surrendering fate to conditions.

Media of all kinds is toxic to the independent mind. Social media could be accelerating the downfall civilization for the conformity it breeds. But those who fear independence and accountability flock to media, particularly social media, for external identity validation. They hope to find Nirvana, within which they can be anesthetized from responsibility for their decisions and their actions. But, at last, there is no escape. Like morphine, the drug of identity requires ever greater doses to the addicted. The eventuality is recognition that it is all an illusion. No chord of human understanding was ever struck. Wisdom itself was denied in pursuit of entertainment. But, in ignorance, there is no escape from wisdom. And the ignorance plagues the possessor just as wisdom elevates her. Certainty requires alignment with the central purpose that is deeply embedded and inherent in an individual — the person's destiny.

9.5 — The Word is "No"
"No" is the word of Certainty. From birth, my brain, and all brains, are saturated by millions of problems and tasks that compel them into tacit compliance and accommodation. As we grow up, we try fighting against our parents and cultural pressures to conform.

At 14, I felt at war with the world around me. I was the "new kid" in 9th grade at Pennbrook Junior High School. Tommy Besch was a tough, pig-faced kid who made it his mission to make my life miserable. Every time I'd pass him in the hall he'd swerve over and bump into me or give me a shove. Now, I was an introverted kid who generally avoided others, which is probably what made me a target. What Tommy didn't know was I was a very angry kid from a dirt road who

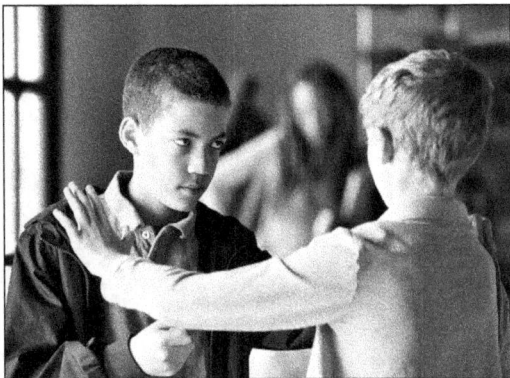

had grown up working hard and playing harder. My family had recently disintegrated in a bad divorce, and I was spoiling for someone to blame for all the crap that had caused. One morning, as I was leaving gym class, I walked right into Tommy Besch, who gave me a book-scattering shove so hard that I hit the deck. Something snapped. All I recall is the word "No," followed by the thought that if I broke that pig nose it would put an end to my troubles with Tommy. The rest is a blur except that I began hammering that pig-faced nose until he couldn't get off the floor. Finally, Coach Crawford parted the crowd, and pulled me off bloodied Tommy.

Something changed that day. Besch was the first of several fights I'd have into my early 20s. I don't condone fighting, but connecting the dots backwards I can see I was frustrated and fed up with the fear. "No" was the only antidote. Nothing, even if it meant a busted face or a smashed hand, was worth submitting to constant cowardice. "No" meant neither God nor man was going to keep me from ridding myself of the knot of uncertainty in my gut.

Certainty must be fought for, and fought for hard. TCP revealed to me that there is nothing, not even life itself, that justifies a brain state of fear or regret. One "No" is worth a thousand "Yeses." "No" is the "full-metal-jacket," the destroyer of doubt and uncertainty. It signals my brain that wisdom, not wimpiness, commands of my domain of control, and that its main job, its only job really, is discovering the solutions that deliver on the mandate that I am destined to fulfill. NΩ

CHAPTER 10
ID IS FOR IDENTITY:
—— DEPOSE MY IDENTITY ——

"A man wrapped up in himself makes a very small package."
FRANKLIN

If I am reliant on external validation for my decisions, I cannot think for myself, and uncertainty grows. I may be under the illusion that I am internally directed, but when the illusion is confronted with the reality, the illusion wins. This is the massive gap between *knowing* the right thing and *doing* the right thing. The disconnection between knowledge and action is always, 100 percent of the time, caused by the desire to preserve and inflate identity. Laziness and passivity are identity-preserving diseases. Neglecting my problems that need solving, or my tasks that need doing, is an act of omission with the purpose of preserving my identity's status quo. If I encounter a person on the street who is hurt, and I act, I am responding appropriately to reality, not necessarily thinking about what the payoff will be to me.

Though I may feel good about my actions later, the motive at the time is "Help!" However, if I (unnaturally) fail to act, I must justify my inaction at the time of the encounter, and then I must continue to do so by building my inaction into a story about myself (identity) that makes my inaction the right choice.

"He probably deserved it. I'm better than him." (see "*schaden-freude*," page 47). Worse yet, I may create a masochistic justification: "I'm an insensitive coward, therefore, I assume no responsibility for helping him."

Such inflations of identity keep growing as long as I allow my identity a position of supremacy. Self-centric behavior is the brain's abstraction of the survival instinct (see "Paramecium Brain," Sec. 5.2), and the root cause of identity crisis, anxiety, and neurotic behavior. Children cry for attention, with the instinct of helpless baby birds in the nest. "I want! Feed me!" How else to avoid demise in the hostile environment that is entirely conditional. In animals, maturity rapidly resolves into autonomy and ever greater levels of control over their environment. This primordial "adulting instinct" eclipses dependencies, and promotes focus, autonomy, humility, and self-reliance. Just observe a hawk soaring — a metaphor for certainty.

Natural selection prohibits animals from remaining dependent, but my brain has evolved to sustain this dependency through identity. The bird who fails to leave the nest, dies. But society (my herd) generally overlooks my unnatural desire to be personally validated long after I should have taken full responsibly and abandoned my fixation with feeding my vanity. Identity-seeking is a measure of my brain's reluctance to abandon this dependency state. It is an act of will to choose my values, to establish my mandate, and, most important, to plan and take action consistent with both. Easier to defer to a vain reliance on judging and the judgment of others, and

the constant partisan comparison to externals that keeps me safely "in the identity nest." Enthrallment with identity (vanity) is my brain flailing in the nest for childlike recognition.

10.1 - Identity is the Brain Thinking Itself

The eye seeing itself is cataract, the ear hearing itself is tinnitus, the stomach digesting itself is peptic ulcer, and the brain thinking of itself is identity. My identity is the

aggregate of all the stories my brain attaches to itself in an effort to give itself meaning. Logic is the brain's function of dividing and solving for a living. But since it can't solve itself, i.e., it cannot reason its own existence, it fabricates meaning through identity. This task is like trying to discover a mathematical formula explaining the phenomenon of mathematics. It's an endless do-loop. Identity is an endless loop of processing experience and attaching emotionally to the output to fabricate a self. But, just as turning a video camera on a monitor, or a microphone on a speaker, causes feedback distortion, the brain's attachment to identity is a reality-distorting experience.

> *Subjectify: to identify with a subject or interpret in terms of subjective experience.*
> MERRIAM-WEBSTER

> Use: *"Taste is a subjective sense that can only truly be distinguished by the one who is doing the tasting."*

Subjectification of reality is the brain's method of managing the torrent of data flow and choice-making that is constantly presented to it though the senses. Logically, my brain eases its workload of problems and tasks by rapidly pigeon-holing new data by its apparent similarities to old data. Subjectification is like the signal-processing filter that's widely used in electronics.

Driving down a familiar street, my brain tends to filter for novelty, disregarding the familiar background. Sometimes we come to ignore the passing scenery altogether, arriving at work unable to recall any details of getting there.

Subjectification can be misleading, particularly when the familiar route I find myself on is the avenue of my own identity. Everything begins to feel the same when my experiences are constantly filtered and reinterpreted to comply with my relentless preoccupation with self. My prejudices — the brain's tendency to over subjectify experience — can trigger reflexive judgments that become habitual, even dominating my ability to reason. Over time, the habit of reliance on subjectified experience results in erroneous generalizations that distort decision-making. "All millennials . . ." or "all boomers . . ." statements, for example, are, of course, irrational, but once they're programmed by habit they can easily trigger erroneous decision-making about any particular millennial or boomer.

A special case occurs when my brain subjectifies itself. As the brain accumulates and fabricates judgments about itself from a constant flow of thoughts about itself, it creates a grand subjectified illusion called "identity."

External data that is contrary to my identity story presents problems that the brain must resolve. That's hard work. Righteousness is easier. It insulates me from exposure to uncomfortable realities that would otherwise mold and shape my reasoning over time.

Identity formation tends to be binary:

- Things that reinforce my identity are good and are incorporated.

- Things that are contrary to my identity are bad and are rejected or, more commonly, attacked, thus further reinforcing my righteousness.

The brain creates a false sense of certainty by isolating itself from external experience through a well-galvanized identity.

But identity-building is like audio feedback. My brain runs reactive identity-reinforcing loops such as: "Wow, she's awesome!" about some celebrity I like, or "God, he's an idiot!" about someone cutting in line, based on how these reactions justify my story about myself, even though such judgments should prompt a rational red flag.

How do I know this is true? My brain clings to such simple irrationals because they are habitual, even if afflictive. This is the "Stockholm Syndrome" of self-seeking. Lacking the effort to see the truth, my brain loops these and thousands of other familiar stories about itself, resonating in the familiar echo chamber where it is held captive. Entrapped, I learn to love my own identity, no matter how onerous, restrictive, or even self-destructive it becomes. Placing a microphone in front of a loudspeaker creates a feedback loop, which in time distorts all sound coming from the speaker until it is inaudible. Similarly, as my brain seeks to define itself (an impossibility). It creates a reality-distorting loop called "identity."

Experiences become abstractions of reality, not reality itself. My subjective identity that "I'm not a sports guy" prevents me from enjoying the excitement of competitive sports because it would conflict with my identity. Subjectivity causes me to handicap outcomes in such a way to reinforce (gain emotional gratification) coherence with my identity. Since all outcomes are fundamentally conditional, identity reinforcement through attachment to outcomes is predictably disappointing, even to the point of feeling victimized.

Outcomes incoherent with my identity can elicit powerful reactions. Consider the highly emotional identity-politics that drove the emotionally charged behaviors in the 2016 U.S. presidential election. A new study shows that for 25 percent of young adults who were given a psychological assessment, the 2016 election race between Donald Trump and Hillary Clinton caused symptoms often seen in those with post-traumatic stress disorder. (Hagan & Sladek, 2018). This identity-outcome dependency can become so compelling that outcomes, no matter how troubling, are interpreted as identity-reinforcing. An example is the *schadenfreude* phenomenon — taking pleasure (identity reinforcement) in the misfortunes of others. When passing a car accident, there's a tendency for the brain to experience an "at least it's not me" sense of justification, rather than dealing with the more realistic, but uncomfortable, sympathetic response. This behavior seeks to preserve identity by seeking validation from even the most unfortunate, even despicable, circumstances. The distortion caused by the subjectified reality drives a desire to make decisions based on what reinforces my little internal reality, and, not coincidentally, the tendency to objectify, judge, and label others.

Objectify: to treat as an object
MERRIAM-WEBSTER

Use: "They believe that beauty pageants objectify women."

The identity's desire to protect itself through the objectification of certain "others" can be leveraged to horrendous consequences.

> *"…biological and racial discourse was becoming part of the taken-for-granted frame of reference <identity> by which the German populace comprehended the different groups who were the victims of the Nazi's objectifying practices."*
> MILCHMAN & ROSENBERG , 1998

10.2 — Deposing Identity

Depose (verb): to remove from a position of power, esp. from a throne; to oust.

Deposing identity requires the skill to check my reflexive tendency to make subjective comparisons in decision-making for the purpose of feeling "special" about myself and my choices. As in chess, the process of deposing the king requires a robust plan of play. My identity is my opponent, and after years invested in acquiring its supremacy, to win takes planning and practice.

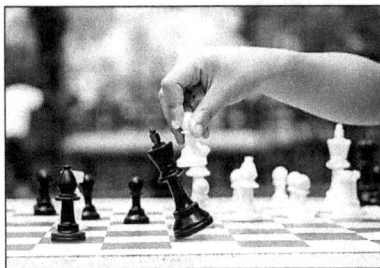

Attack and Deflect are two fundamentals in chess strategy, and they are also the two forces of will for deposing identity.

Attacking means first having an offensive strategy then developing a mastery for quick evaluation and action on problems, tasks, and opportunities that invariably present themselves. My plan follows from my mandate. Without goals I cannot defeat the distractions compelled by my identity. Mastering action comes from knowledge and skills development. Absent learning the skills required to execute on my mandate, conditions will take control and I will become frustrated and discouraged.

"To know and to act are one and the same"
YANGMING, 1996

Deflection in chess is anticipation of your opponent's next moves, and playing against them to thwart the attack. Learning to say "No" to external options, and, more importantly, to my "self"-sustaining internal dialog, is key to the identity defense. If I know that I will be distracted from my work by my e-mail compulsion, I must shut it off. If a friend or family member tends to draw me into "identity-centric" gossip, or judgmental and opinionated conversations about conditional subject matter, I must shut them off. If I find myself becoming emotionally enthralled in my own righteousness, I must shut myself off! Discerning between what is wanted and what is needed is key. I must deflect what is wanted so I can embrace and focus on what is needed.

10.3 — Self
"There comes a time when every good man must wear a mask."
THE LONE RANGER

Where is my "self"? Precisely where is located? What does it look like? What is its weight and volume? I can identify the location of my heart, my brain and my liver, but not myself, because self, *per se*, does not exist. All adherence to "selfs" — selfishness, self image, self esteem, self consciousness, etc. — are versions of the brain's enthrallment with trying to label and conceptualize its own function in the same manner as it habitually pigeonholes everything else. In an endless cycle of identity-seeking, identity is brain masturbation. Whether the result of such enthrallment is inflation — "I am great." — or deprecation — "I suck." — the myopic perspective, over time, is isolating. The effect on reasoning is distortion. At its worst, it leaves me incapable of unbiased, or even rational, decision making. The brain's novelty-seeking need to habituate, i.e., to relegate common experiences and sensory input into the background, also applies to the identity illusion. As we mature and our brains adopt a particular identity as real, it habituates that identity and seeks data that reinforces it.

Facebook leverages such self-seeking vanity. Casual identity is benign enough. But as identity begins to dominate, even enthrall my thinking, it enables a compulsive attachment to identity that becomes addictive and destructive. Addiction to identity — to the externally focused definition of self — can't end well because external conditions will always fall short of the expectations of an inflated identity, and reinforce the expectations of the victim identity. The key to certainty is not abandoning identity. It is learning that identity is an illusion, a game. What is my "self"? There is none!

10.4 — Identity Cold Turkey

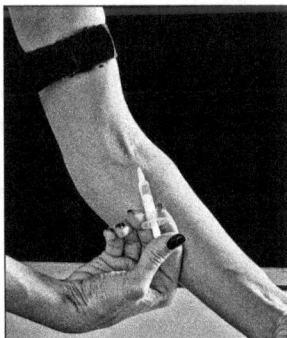

Escaping identity-addiction is an act of willpower, but there is a trick. Simply put, it's developing the mindset that identity is irrational, not because there are no answers to be found, but because, fundamentally, there is no "searcher" to be found. Identity is the brain's pattern-recognition logic trying to create a pattern image (story) of its own pattern recognition system. Like holding a camera up to a monitor, the result is feedback. Such identity-seeking feedback loops are accompanied by emotional hooks such as righteousness, pride, fear, regret, etc. These are the "juice" that reinforces the process as meaningful.

Depression is an example of entrapment in such a negative loop, but grandiosity is a different flavor of the same poison. This echo chamber of identity-reinforcement can become a comfortable, if not neurotic, place to hide from reality. Whether such emotional juicing is positive or negative is secondary to the impact of the illusion, which is reliably disappointing.

Recognizing that "there's no there, there" with respect to "self" is a simple, first step. But acquiring the skills to check habitual attachment to the illusion of self takes work. This hard work overcomes the addiction to a lifetime of identity-driven emotional "fixes." Again, we experience *schadenfreude* — the joy experienced at another's misfortune (van Dijk, van Koningsbruggen, & Ouwerkerk, 2011). It is pure identity-enhancing emotional brain play that inhibits the feeling of compassion, that uncomfortable, but natural, human (perhaps even animal) response to suffering. In contrast the joy experienced in the unconditional love of a child, for example, like compassion is selfless. Identity-based emotionality begins evaporating once the illusion of identity is exposed and debunked.

10.5 — Why Identity?
Identity-seeking behaviors result from the reflexive cycle of thought and its related emotion. Emotionally charged thoughts of any kind can evolve into a dependency in similar fashion to the way drugs can elicit an emotional response and become psychologically addictive. The morphine high becomes cognitively connected with the drug, the needle, the fix. Similarly, sadness and melancholy that results from the compulsive "victimism" reinforces my thinking that I am a victim. That reinforces the sadness, and the brain pushes out serotonin on the validation. "At least I have my misery" is not

an uncommon response from someone addicted to a victim mentality. I might wonder why one would perpetuate such a cycle. I suggest that the incidence of any emotion reinforces that at least I have an identity, when identity has come to define my existence.

In a culture where identity is the primary tool for driving consumption, those lacking enough internal definition are easy targets. Unless the game is recognized for what it is, those who are susceptible absorb such external influences (advertising, media, celebrity) as important parts of their identity, especially during periods that are economically or politically disruptive. Clinically this is the definition of the depressive state.

Fundamentally, I am desperate for identity in the absence of a logical explanation for my existence. An illusion of experience results that can become so predominant that it becomes my substitute for real experience. Over time this habit becomes so compelling that I go to extremes to sustain it — albeit afflictive — selectively resisting exposure to fact in favor of the safety of the illusion. The brain's existential uncertainty is the motive force of identity formation. The experience of "clinging" or "attachment" to such an identity becomes a substitute for the experience of reality, with inherent consequences. The resulting attachment to the thought<=>emotion loop consumes bandwidth, and limits my experience of the present. As mentioned above, the distorted isolation tends to prevent me from decisions that are based on fact. Instead it promotes a "cogni-motive" (thinking emotive loop) shelter that promotes decisions and actions based on emotion rather than reason.

Identity is the aggregation of multiple cogni-motive cycles, which run into the thousands. These cycles run at various levels of the brain's operating system in a similar manner that software runs on a computer. Some loops, or "threads," are small and may be conscious or unconscious — variously surfacing from time to time. Some are very influential, likewise operating at a conscious level or not. The character of these loops may be virtuous, assistive, benign, and afflictive, depending on the level and type of impact with which they effect behavior. But one thing they have in common is this: They consume the brain's bandwidth, and, as such, these aggregate running loops crowd out conscious attention until it is no longer functioning adequately. Reasoning slows in a similar manner as a computer processor.

The "understanding gap" between my ability to hear what a person is saying and understand what the person is trying to communicate, depends on my ability to neutralize my own cogni-motive loops (CM-Loops). Emotional intelligence is a function of such brain de-looping. But this isn't the only limitation that is conferred by such loops. CM Loops insulate me from reality by distorting the lens through which I experience my life. At a minimum they prejudice my experience, and at worst they insulate me from experience altogether.

Such prejudicial loops are often associated with fear. It isn't the purpose of this work to deeply investigate the nature or relevance of these loops. Rather the purpose is to implicate them as the primary source of poor judgment. Learning and skill development presumably enable the refinement and elevation of judgment. Egoic loops of all types serve to inhibit judgment, and, at the extreme, can occlude the capacity for rational judgment altogether. Chronic looping results in depressive personality when brain bandwidth is consumed by CM-Loops to the point that they become my reality.

10.6 — Reality Shatters Identity

Humans can exist in a benign state of chronic CM-Looping aka, identity. These loops, or stories, accumulated and reinforced from childhood — compelled by the brain's distorted enthrallment with the accumulation of acknowledgments — are often self-reinforced to the point that the loops take on the false perception of a reality all their own. In effect, I am in an illusion comprised of my CM-Loops.

I'm a vegan. I'm a conservative. I'm an intellectual. Each of identities come with an adherent set of stories that explain and justify each facet of my identity. But the identity I carry around with me is a synthesis based loosely on past events conflated with justifications based on my fears and aspirations. However, since no illusion can stand up to reality, confrontation with experience incoherent with the illusion can shatter one or more of my brain's stories about itself, a difficult, even painful, event. Getting fired, divorced, the death of a loved one, or confrontation with one's own death can unravel even the most robust identity. The resulting "identity crisis" leads, for better or for worse, to the dissolution of the important stories making up the illusion.

10.7 — Fear & Regret

I got fired. As a teenager, I had started out as a laborer on the fishing piers of San Francisco. Over the next 30 years I rose through the ranks, put myself through college, followed by a series of management roles. By the time I was approaching my mid-50s I was a proud CEO of an important firm, and my self-identity was set. I was someone who tenaciously fought his way to the top, and that was reinforced by external achievement and an internal dialog that inflated my factually modest accomplishment with the justification that my success was more than deserved. I could go where I wanted, and do what I wanted. I was pushy and aggressive because my identity told me I was right. I was to be listened to, and I sure needn't listen to others. Though this illusion was failing me, I didn't know how or why. But my trajectory was dropping. Then I was fired.

Even though I was aware that there were business issues, nothing prepared me for the true impact of being fired. A business I'd invested myself in all my life had kicked me out. I was devastated. During the long ride home, my identity began unraveling in my head. I'd gone from a Somebody to a Nobody in less time than it took to drive from New York to Philadelphia. As I was pulling into my driveway, I was struggling with how I would explain it to my family, to my wife. I was afraid, and I was beginning to reject my arrogant illusion of identity.

All CM-Loops eventually wind up at fear and regret. Therefore, dissolving such illusions is necessary to restore the childlike lightness of the unencumbered brain. One solution is to develop a skill for trying along. That is, rather than being willful, I free my brain to give each experience its fair weight, without allowing my identity's thumb to tilt the scale. My responses become more accurate and proportional. When I surrender self-perception as my lens on reality, and learn to perceive things as they really are, it relaxes my approach to living. Developing an understanding that there is no separate "I" to defend — that there is only the manifesting experience — is the first step in such learning.

10.8 — My Face

The massive success of Facebook, LinkedIn, and other social media platforms is fueled, in large part, by the powerful influence that identity holds over me as part of the herd. If I already have a vain attachment to personal image, why not put it on line for all the world to see — and "like"? Neurology that begins with physical survival evolves into identity survival. If I fail to see that identity is merely a game my brain is playing on itself, what other perceived "facts" are, likewise, delusional?

10.9 — Killing Vanity

"When dealing with people, remember you are not dealing with creatures of logic, but with creatures bristling with prejudice, and motivated by pride and vanity."
CARNEGIE, 1936

Vanity is enthrallment with personal identity. It is the brain's insulation from reality. Typically, the struggles required in completing the countless tasks that are mandated by greater horizons of achievement, forges personal transformation that is vanity-defeating.

But, if I am enthralled with my identity, why bother changing? It is far easier to inflate, embellish, and justify my behaviors than to change them. But vanity is delusional, ultimately inhibiting to achievement.

> *"The Tyrant is a child of Pride*
> *Who drinks from his sickening cup of Recklessness and Vanity,*
> *Until from his high crest headlong*
> *He plummets to the Dust of Hope."*
> SOPHOCLES, 429 BC

When the vain person finally "plummets," it doesn't come without warning. Like a good movie, the dangers of identity-obsession are foreshadowed, if one is paying attention. The subtle and not-so-subtle signs of impending trouble tend to show up as a "getting stuckness" that produces a sensation of inertia, frustration, fatigue, and even depression. NΩ

CHAPTER 11
ACQUIRING
——— CERTAINTY BEHAVIOR ———

Mastering my reality through certainty is more physics than philosophy. Acquiring effective skills is as simple as replacing software on a computer, just not as easy when the computer is my brain. Reprogramming a computer is mostly automatic. Reprogramming my brain is a conscious skill-acquisition process, requiring 1.) awareness that uncertainty is the problem, 2.) practice at eliminating the old mindset, and 3.) practice at habituating the new mindset.

Practice is the difference. To hit three pointers consistently in basketball, I need first to decide to do it, then learn to stop shooting *at* the basket while learning to shoot *into* the basket. My decision to master the long game is to practice visualizing the ball in the basket before the shot, while erasing the old habit of "just shooting." Likewise, adopting The Certainty Principle requires both my intolerance to the signs of uncertainty in my life, and the will power to eliminate and replace the mindset that is causing it.

Signs of Uncertainty	TCP Element	Eliminate	Replace
Getting Nowhere Chronic feeling of being stuck	**Forever Horizon**	**Short-term perspective.** Become aware of, and reduce, hasty and impatient behaviors.	Focus on seeing the long-term benefit of your goals and actions. Study and mimic the lives of those who have had a sustaining, positive impact.

Signs of Uncertainty	TCP Element	Eliminate	Replace
Purposelessness Chronic feeling of personal and existential meaninglessness	**Mandate**	**Dreaming** about what others have or do. Ignoring my talents and skills regardless of how I think they appear to others.	Accountability. My individual meaning is to solve problems and complete tasks that are constantly presented, while discovering and executing my mandate.
Irresponsibility Lack of conscientiousness and integrity.	**Income**	**Avoid** of facts and figures that score the results of my efforts in terms of benchmarks and personal bests.	Measuring and monitoring incomes that account the progress of my mandate.
Fear and Regret Chronic worry about the future, and regret about past events.	**Outcome**	**Outcome dependence.** Outcomes are mainly conditional. Surrender emotional attachment to them. Do not cling to getting personal meaning from the way things turn out.	All outcomes are pointers which may or may not be any of my responsibility. Take relevant outcome data points and use them to "connect the dots," pointing to my next action steps.
Chronic Self-Talk Constant comparison and judgment of self and others	**Identity**	**Résumé Identity** is an illusion. Actively demote and eliminate vanity-based thinking of all kinds.	Promote "other-centered" conversations. Focus on action. I am only as valuable my present actions serving my mandate.

CHAPTER 12
BIG BRAIN ORGAN

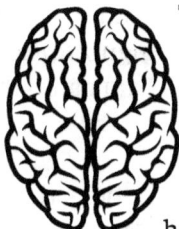

The brain, through which all reality data is processed, is an organ that deals with certainty and uncertainty in the same way that the stomach deals with hunger and satiety. But the brain is a loud and hungry organ. It's like a set of small intestines in our head in constant need of feeding — hounding me constantly to be fed.

When I am hungry my stomach growls, and I seek any food that will satisfy it. When I am full it digests the nutrients that reinforce my body. When I am uncertain (e.g., fearful) my brain seeks to abstract the data it takes in from the senses to comfort itself. When I am certain (e.g., confident) it abstracts the data to reinforce my concept of self. As a device, the brain's limitations are defined by its binary operating system. Cognition is the brain's game, which is to say the BOSS (Brain's Operating Symbolic System) is coded for the cognition game — deciphering certainty vs. uncertainty by naming experiences with words. This binary brain game seeks certainty through comparison. Coke or Pepsi? Boxers or briefs? War or Peace?

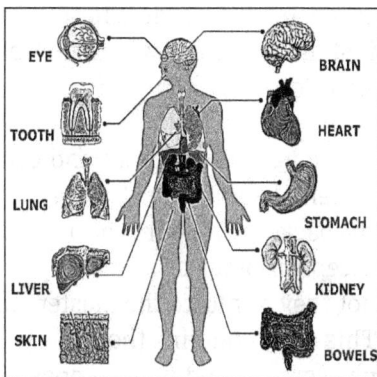

But is this BOSS game the only game? Is reality as I experience it filtered through the BOSS, reducing my interpretation of reality to mere "... shadows on the wall," as Plato describes in "The Republic"?

Furthermore, the stories that my brain creates about me to establish certainty through identity (RAPPs: Repetitive Auto-reinforcing Personification Programs) further filter day-to-day reality to the point of gray distortion, even fantasy, about what is really going on around me. Ironically, clinging to such stories feeds the very demon of self from which I am naturally trying to escape.

Nearly every waking hour, my brain seeks emotion-stimulating data patterns. We sometimes call these "stories," and the brain is a story-making machine. From the moment we awaken (and sometimes even while we sleep) our brains are on a voracious hunt for stories with conclusions, creating the input/emotion connection that it finds so satisfying. As children, the fabric of our personal stories is thin, and there are many windows that allow us to experience life in an unencumbered way. That is to say, life is experienced "*de novo*" — instant by instant with little coloring or attachment to prior experience.

As we age, these stories and connections become richer and richer. At some stage this aggregate "epic story" takes over as the backdrop for our conscious experience. And we may begin accepting or rejecting real experiences based upon whether or not they reinforce the master story line created by our brain. This story contains thousands of biases that may or may not be accurate, and may be operating on the conscious or subconscious level of brain activity. Often when the story becomes mature a phenomenon known as "confirmation bias" can evolve to dominate our field of perception. It's all fueled by the brain's insatiable desire to reinforce the stories running in its neurons — in its RAM, to extend the computer analogy. At extreme, the narrowness of viewpoint becomes my identity. It becomes the internal definition of my very existence, to the exclusion of true existence. Again, this is Plato's "Allegory of the Cave." The illusion takes over, and experience is only the "shadows on the wall," the remnants of the filters and mutation of the true manifesting reality. Such fabrications clearly are counterproductive, so what is the solution to the certainty-and-confidence dilemma?

Just as the stomach is the organ of food digestion, the brain is the organ of data digestion. It is effective in reasoning with known sensory data, but its effectiveness declines as the data becomes abstracted. Reasoning, or cognition, is the brain's domain of certainty synthesis, but it is a domain with limitations. Formal and informal logic is the cognitive "software" of reasoning — mathematics being its purest form. But logic is optimal for solving problems that are non-abstracted (real, concrete). Logic is the algorithm of the brain, not the algorithm of the universe of all problems, and herein lies the rub. Problems that are beyond the logical domain create uncertainties that are often rationalized through theories, conjecture, and the fabrication of the stories that define us. The more abstract and persistent the target of cognitive activity, the more uncertain the brain becomes, and the more embedded the stories become. Uncertainty encumbers action-taking, and so effects performance in a variety of negative ways, causing inflexibility and reactivity. Just as bad food causes indigestion that preoccupies the experience with gastrointestinal distress, uncertainty undermines performance by eroding confidence, a key predictor of progress. More so, because experience (sensory data collection) is localized in the brain (the very organ of reality perception) it becomes difficult to distinguish between the fabrications brought about by chronic uncertainty and those that come from reality itself. The brain's stories bring relief to uncertainty by creating identity.

Identity formation is the brain's process of synthesizing certainty. It creates the illusion that abstract thoughts are reality, and it centers such thoughts (stories) around the thinker. Consider a compliment or criticism you might have received as a child. After all, "I" is the sole common denominator in a universe of uncertainty. Therefore "I" is the natural germ of certainty around which stories can be attached to provide rational meaning — to provide certainty. The identity illusion insulates the brain from the onslaught of reality data that is constantly impinging upon it.

Consider the phenomenon of identification with celebrities. Steve Jobs, Warren Buffett, the Kardashians. Their stories all provide respite from the harsh sensory data of my reality by co-opting someone else's story who is rich, famous, and successful. I can reinforce the illusion through all manner of activity: reading their twitter feeds and buying their clothes or cologne. Celebrities often thrive on the attachment of their fans, capitalizing on it for their own benefit. Such fantasies are double illusions because I am fabricating an illusion about a relationship with an abstracted perception of an individual that's been fabricated by their publicist. Such attachments promote inaction, as the aggregate fixation with such fantasies consume bandwidth that would otherwise be mandate-directed.

Identity creation is the brain seeking certainty through an illusion rather than reality. This process is enhanced when reality becomes particularly uncomfortable. Children frequently prefer such illusions, creating imaginary worlds and friends when the real world becomes too uncomfortable. But identity is not reality. It is a "safe space" where one can hide from reality.

Adults who adopt their stories (loose recollections of past events conflated with various facts and fictions) as their identities find their ability to deal objectively with reality diminished. When my brain reverts to identity as primary truth, I reflexively seek external inputs that reinforce the illusion. Again, my "confirmation bias" dominates.

Plato's "The Allegory of the Cave" (Plato, 380 BC) addresses how the illusion of identity can dominate our perceptions to the point where experience becomes little more than watching shadows on the wall. He contrasts the flat, colorless illusion in the cave of our identity with the rich, multi-dimensional world of instantaneous experience — of vast horizons. But the "cave" of identity has no horizon. It is home to the stories born of fear and regret that, with constant repetition (cognitive reinforcement), become familiar, and, therefore, perversely comforting. Beyond the "cave" are the unfamiliar and vast horizons of possibility, unique for each of us. But they are only accessible if we can free ourselves from the chains of identity holding us prisoner.

12.1 — Human Brain Fails Turing Test

In principle, the Turing Test anticipates a future when the behaviors of artificial intelligence will evolve to be indistinguishable from human behaviors (Turing, Computing Machinery and Intelligence, 1950). But does my brain, left to its own devices, fundamentally reflect what it means to be human, or is there something much deeper and more essential to the quality of existence?

For example, imagine your computer flashing messages on its screen bragging about how great it is, and with each headline came a little picture story justifying that assertion.

"I am amazing! Did you see the way I ran that PowerPoint™ presentation for you with the little animated jumping dog? Doesn't this make you feel even more appreciative of my part in your life and how important I am? It's my CPU, isn't it brilliant".

Or the opposite: "I'm so sorry I locked up on that spreadsheet. Geez, I'm an idiot!"

Or what if the CPU suddenly began reporting its own reactive judgments about external data that came up in its browser.

"Oh, I think that woman's TED Talk on effective communication is worthless, what an idiot!" Or, "In my opinion, that guy's YouTube on fitness training is ridiculous. What a jerk!"

And if such a computer could evolve, its CPU might become so engaged with judgments (based on its own comparative identity) that it could begin losing the impartial objectivity and vast "perspective" that I rely on for, say, the accuracy of a Google search, or the computation in a spreadsheet. What if it doesn't like the answers it generates? Will it alter the facts to fit its own pre-conceived notion of the truth?

As the machine seeks to justify its own existence, its value as a task-directed tool that helps me evaluate problems, calculate accurately, and boost productivity could become increasingly distorted, eventually co-opting my individual priorities altogether. In time, "machine vanity" might become integrated and controlling. It might become the central driver of my priorities and values. Like "HAL" in "2001: A Space Odyssey," the survival of such Artificial Intelligence identity could result in malevolent machines that marginalize humanity altogether.

Rather than pursuing individual mandates that I know to be accurate and important, I might default to obey the distractions of the device. Eventually I might default my will, and mindlessly follow the machine, subverting personal priorities and goals to it as it becomes increasingly enthralled with spinning the facts to support its own self-image, rather than mandates as simple as right and wrong. Does this sound familiar?

Thinking Is Abstraction

Like a computer, the uncertain brain habitually fabricates stories about itself that reinforce existing stories, because the brain is a division-seeking, pattern-recognizing, security-fabricating organ. It "self-incentivizes," extracting gratification from the process of division and dot-connection that are fundamental to the various games of survival. When the game is "self" survival, this objective is called Identity.

Identity is the game the brain plays to rationalize (division and comparison) its own existence. As we will see, this game is impossible to win through reasoning, because consciousness is non-cognitive. Thinking about what is real can/will only produce a symbolic representation of reality, but is not the human experience of reality. Refined reasoning (mathematics, for example) abstracts and argues explanations of objective reality with high, though never absolute, accuracy. But, my brain's preoccupation with thoughts about its subjective self can easily slip free from the constraints of logic. As my unbridled, self-centered brain seeks gratification, it accumulates and fabricates facts willy-nilly for its own embellishment, its own self-justification.

Does the brain really fail itself each time it meanders off into the identity domain? Yes, but that's only problematic if I am unconscious of such departures from reality. Identity is a deceptively simple brain game because there are no rules beyond the consequences that creep up on me from a pattern of such unconscious self-delusion. Obesity results from a habit of gorging on food in unconscious denial of the consequences. Gratification in the feeding my own persona, and failure to engage objectively in fact, results in an identity-obesity that is equally unhealthy. Four fifths of all drivers feel they are above average, an example referred to as "Illusory Superiority" (Hoorens, 1993). Through Identity my brain creates its own gold standard, and this standard is often so distorted that it overwhelms logic.

12.2 — The Dunning-Kruger Effect

The cognitive bias with which the human brain assesses reality — particularly self-assessment and self-competency — is known as The Dunning-Kruger (DKE) effect. The phenomenon observed by Dunning and Kruger was that most individ-

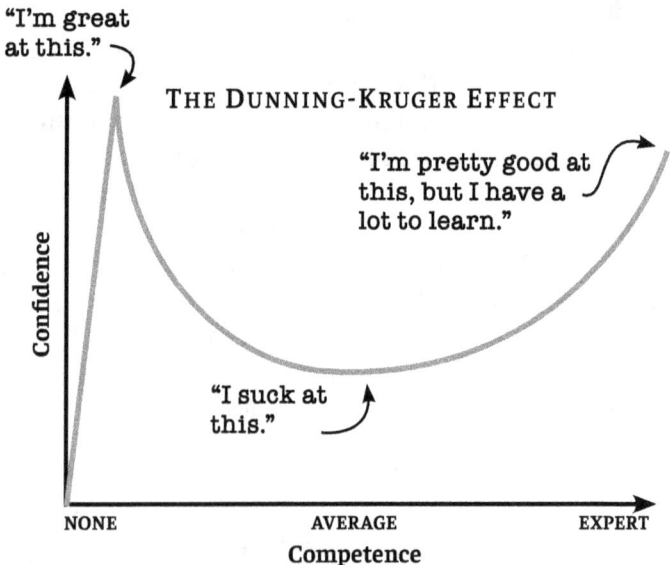

THE DUNNING-KRUGER EFFECT

"I'm great at this."

"I'm pretty good at this, but I have a lot to learn."

"I suck at this."

Confidence

NONE   AVERAGE   EXPERT

Competence

uals are unable to objectively evaluate their own competencies (Justin & Dunning, 1999). Now, if (upon reading this) you find your internal voice saying...

"Of course, that's 'most people,' but I am not most people"

... your identity's desperate need to self-justify is, in fact, validating the DKE hypothesis. All observations are distorted through the lens of Identity, particularly self-observation. There is no escaping the distortion, save detaching myself from the biases I have accumulated over time known collectively as Identity.

The dangers of DKE-driven identity are obvious. When identity rules reason, differing opinions are reflexively rejected. *Ad hominem* identity-based judgments dominate choices that would otherwise be based on objective evaluations of an individual's actions and arguments. Facts are distorted to fit the identity narrative in my head. Of all human behaviors, then, is identity maintenance really the intelligent use of the brain's certainty-seeking function? Or, is identity just the easy, low-risk way of insulating myself from the immense uncertainty of the external world. Furthermore, does the brain's enthrallment with identity inhibit intelligent human behavior?

The Turing Test evaluates if a machine's ability to exhibit intelligent behavior is indistinguishable from that of a human. This leads to the question: What is intelligent human behavior? Which human behaviors are intelligent, and which are not?

In The Certainty Principle, I make the assumption that human behaviors driven by reasoning are intelligent, and that behaviors driven by identity-seeking are not. Further, I define

Identity as my brain's tendency to create and conflate stories about itself to fill the void of inscrutability of its own meaning.

My anger at not winning the lottery, even though I am a good, hard working person who's bought many tickets, may be a good story, and even sound justified. But it is not good reasoning. My categorical judgment of a person based on, say, their political views, may feel right, but is reliably irrational. A computer exhibiting this kind of behavior might be perceived as a "humanoid," but not an adult humanoid. My laptop becoming petulant or angry when it wasn't getting the bandwidth it desired could be entertaining for a time, but a very short time. My brain passes the Turing Test when the intelligent qualities of the human behavior prevail, characterized by an immunity to the influence of identity seeking. If my laptop's CPU becomes preoccupied with its comparative performance versus others of its species, I have a problem. Should its CPU become enthralled with creating self-deprecating stories about its own inadequacies, I suspect it would lose its value to me altogether.

Why should it be different for my brain?

In effect, I observe some of this behavior already when my computer maintenance programs show me an unhappy face — when its "story" becomes too encumbered by all the stuff accumulated over the course of normal operation. The difference is, I can click a button and my laptop is purged. Unfortunately, my brain lacks such a specific maintenance routine, and "bad code" can run on, unencumbered, without my willful intervention. The stories my brain concocts about itself (masquerading as identity) tend to perpetuate to the point that my interpretation of normal daily experiences become conflated with the stories that my brain has already fabricated about itself. It fills in the memory gaps with pattern formation and, *voilà*, — here's "My Brain's Story of Me." My identity.

Consider my life-long disdain for pistachio ice cream. I am "not a nut person." I have loved peanut butter since childhood, but disliked all other nuts, particularly nuts in ice cream. So, never having tried pistachio (bright green no less), the mere thought of pistachio ice cream seemed, well, especially repulsive. Despite my wife's repeated encouragement to try it, I'd denied myself this green treat for more than 50 years. Once I finally relented, you guessed it. Turned out I love pistachio ice cream.

Ice cream makers aside, my position on pistachio prejudice was of little importance to anyone, save the needless decades of self-imposed exile from nut-land. But the consequences of identification with any position is limiting, even destructive. Delusional self-evaluation (see DKE, above), particularly regarding safety, produces bad outcomes.

In my 40s, I was a heavy drinker. I couldn't get through the day without a bottle in my desk, often draining it before day's end. I identified myself with whiskey, and was convinced I was functionally better for consuming it. I concocted an internal story identifying myself with famous functional drinkers, real and fictional. Ulysses S. Grant. Ernest Hemingway. Alexander the Great. My father. I'd embellish my addiction with stories of heroes who drank and prospered. I did all this right up to the point when, while speeding home on a dark country road, I careened into a ditch mere milliseconds away from running over a child who shot out in front of my car on a bicycle.

Over time my stories become so deeply embedded that they filter and distort my experiences and judgments. Identity run amok can come to dominate reality itself, building me up, tearing me down, or confusing me altogether, based on the prevailing identity of the moment. Be it virtuous or afflictive, once identity dominates, independence and accountability recede, and with them so does my awareness of time and consequence — the measure of which I call "temporal perspective."

12.3 — Certainty Time

The brain only exists in the present, creating a disproportionate sense of urgency over the most trivial issues. Certainty is incoherent with urgency. TCP tells me that a huge temporal frame of reference is primary to certainty creation. A pattern of reactive decisions demotes deliberation, while promoting emotional judgments that erode confidence, well-being, and accountability.

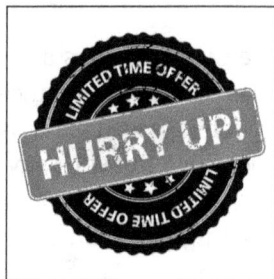

When my foundational perspective of time is essentially infinite, I am at liberty to view my choices as historically consequential. The certainty of a ten-year-old's summer day results from the temporal perspective that each day is a lifetime, and that each activity is historic!

On one such day, in the field above our farm, I saved a baby rabbit whose family had been run over by a tractor. I recall the deeply certain sensation of rescuing and nursing the bunny as a nearly religious experience. The impact of that day echoes even today, and has, no doubt, influenced thousands of subsequent choices. It is testimony to the timelessness of authentic experiences. An identity-free-forever temporal perspective relieves me of my compulsion for instant gratification, replacing it with a deep sense of place and purpose that is otherwise unattainable.

12.4 — Brain Validation

I am born into a domain of vast uncertainty. My brain struggles to create order from the apparent chaos via its pattern-seeking bios. The brain accumulates patterns and conflates and recycles stories about itself, but they are not reality. They are simply the models the brain uses to deal with the uncertainty of its own existence. But the brain can fool itself into adopting its stories as reality.

The illusion that my stories are reality, is my Identity. The brain engages in constant positive and negative reinforcement, a grand confirmation bias, to keep and inflate the elements that define identity. Left unchecked, such identity pattern-seeking enthralls the brain with thousands of stories, repeatedly looping and reinforcing themselves consciously and unconsciously in epic story of identity acknowledgment. These loops consume bandwidth while anchoring me in my stories. This quest for short-term gratification becomes difficult to escape, and I begin to see my identity illusion as reality itself. It's all about myself!

An interesting test of reliance on identity is one's response to acknowledgments by others. Most of us are highly vulnerable to identity acknowledgment, and our choices can be influenced significantly by it. To gain our attention — and our money — much of the advertising that bombards us employs tactical acknowledgment of our identity. Our loves, hates, regrets, and fears are constantly paraded through our brainscapes in search of external data that can be construed as validation. Chronic threat and regret result when our stories dominate and distort reasoning, impeding the struggle to behave intelligently and reasonably. In short, to make accurate choices of action.

12.5 — The Brain Problem

Certainty is what remains when there is no problem. As an uncertainty-seeking device, the brain seeks problems to solve. When the brain engages, a problem exists. If there's no brain engagement, no problem exists.

Problem-seeking, like all seeking, is an uncertainty generating exercise. But brain self-seeking is the origination of identity and ineffectiveness, whereas selfless problem-solving is the mechanics of effectiveness and productivity. Problem-solving is the proper definition of the use of human-cognition faculties. Chasing problems that do not present themselves within my domain of accountability is a waste of time and energy. To satisfy my brain's desire to enhance identity, I seek (not solve) problems that are not mine. This is the origin of virtue signaling. I seek to identify with a problem that is not mine for the purpose of appearances.

Certainty reinforces that my brain has no purpose beyond the inherent mandate I am born to deliver on, based on talent and skill. Neglect my mandate, and I am good for little more than fertilizer.

In an effort to fill the hole that is left from denial of my mandate, I can seek artificial means to demonstrate that I have purpose and meaning when, for example, the occupation I have chosen has none. Because all such identity-reinforcing problem-seeking is delusional, meaning-seeking is a delusional exercise in building up identity with two possible outcomes. If I am alert, foolishness following my folly will lead to humility, because perpetuating the delusion of such vanity will eventually lead me to the illumination that virtue is a verb, not an attribute to be worn like the logo on a cap or a t-shirt. Taking occasional shots of virtue by "wearing ashes" only perpetuates the delusion, leading me to a life of self-righteousness and judgementalism. Virtue mongers understand the vulnerability of the virtue vein and capitalize on it. Religions, for example, leverage the purpose-gap that's created in the lives of those choosing to deny coming to terms with their mandate. But such virtue-signaling always leads to frustration, fear, and anger over the inadequacy of "talking without walking." Only by offering myself up in sacrifice to the work that is my imperative quenches my thirst for meaning, my need for Certainty.

12.6 — Brainwidth

Visual Bandwidth: 300-780nm
Visual Perception: .0001 - 100,000 Lux
Auditory Range: 20-20,000Hz
Auditory Limits: 5-150DB
Haptic Measurement: TPD test: 2.3 mm

There are measurements of olfactory senses based on the ability to perceive, say, orange-flavored Jell-O™. Suffice to say that young people have 50 times the olfactory sensitivity as 70-year-olds. Cognition on the IQ scale ranges from vegetative state to about 200 (normalized to 100).

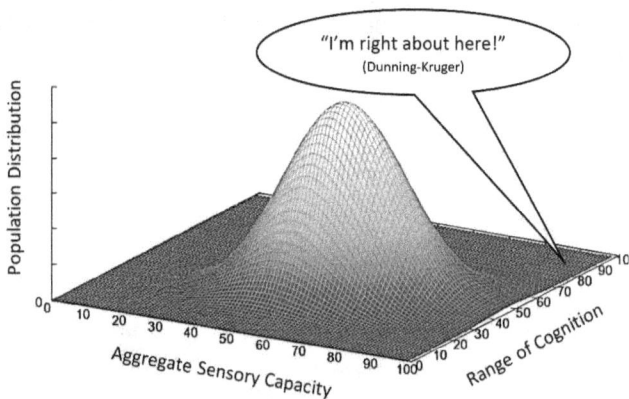

All human sensory ranges are narrow when compared to the entire spectrum of available signal. The above graph represents the "hill" of human experiential capacity. We are all somewhere in that hill. Though we can use tools to improve sensory detection, we cannot materially alter sensory capacity. We are ultimately limited by our ability to "read" these derivative inputs. All are abstractions of the underlying reality (an infra-red photograph shows infra-red wavelengths in, well, red). What is the sound of a 30,000Hz vibration? No human being knows.

Likewise, the brain is a limited computing device. Besides having important recall limitations, its other calibrations of computational capacity are feeble compared to say an Intel Core i7-8700K. Try installing a new piece of brain software with the ease of say Office 365™ on a laptop! But, even the i7 operates on the binary sorting process of the brain. Is it the only form of cognition possible?

So, why do I maintain such righteous reliance on my own perceptions and computations as a determinant of what is possible? No good reason. I am cognitively constrained just as we are "sensorily" constrained. As such, it is all-the-more important that my accurate evaluation of experience is optimized and unencumbered. Despite these limitations I allow unbridled vanity. Even a frog thinks he's a god.

Like any CPU, the brain is limited by its "clock speed," and by clogging the data pipe with useless signal. There is a limited rate at which the brain cycles calculations, and how much data it can reasonably process at a time. Even a computer will stumble with "cloggy" code. Unlike the computer, though, the brain is subject to physical fatigue, which can diminish its processing capacity to that of a gerbil. At its worst, I experience Velcro™ moments, getting stuck in stupid, escalating frustration (identity attachment), and, in turn, accelerating my error rate.

"The brain can only do one thing at a time with excellence…"
COVEY, 1989

Steven R. Covey's statement reflects the limitations of the brain as a CPU. There are limits to multitasking, particularly when the multitasks are trivial.

Abstractions, particularly those connected with repetitive, self-inflicted identity attacks, get reinforced by an emotional load. Messages such as "My third grade teacher told me I would never amount to anything," consume bandwidth more than reason-based, problem-solving activities because they don't succumb to the razor of logical reasoning. Emotion makes data indigestible, and drives logic errors and judgment failures. It creates, in a word, uncertainty.

Logic-intensive games (e.g., solitaire), where subtle judgment errors spell defeat, are important platforms for testing this hypothesis. My judgment suffers when my brain is preoccupied with self-centered, emotional abstractions that consume my capacity for reasoning, i.e., logical decision-making. The greater my preoccupation with emotion-driven, self-centered abstract identity loops, the greater my uncertainty.

12.7 — RAPPs

The brain as a computational device responds rather inefficiently to reprogramming. Adults always have a suite of software running at various levels of complexity. Some whole programs, some apps, some fragments of code — vestiges of a former operating system or particularly significant imprints caused by one trauma or another. The code runs by necessity or because it has insinuated its own feedback loop. Call it RAPP, — Repetitive Auto-reinforcing Personification Programs. These are typically reinforced with emotional (hormonal) attachments, therefore making thoughtless experience more and more difficult to achieve.

RAPPs take all forms, but they all have one trait in common: Reactivity. "He's a jerk!" "She's a genius!"

Stopping RAPPs requires five basic steps.

1. **Label the RAPP** — The next time my brain finds itself sliding into a familiar reactive monologue, quick, name the RAPP. For example, say the RAPP is "Fat people are lazy and selfish." Each time I see an obese person I begin spinning my judgmental story about how disgusting I find fat people. The remedy's first step is to name the RAPP. Here, the "Fat RAPP" is the judgmental recurring story in my head, triggered by encountering someone who is obese. Naming the RAPP is the key first step that enables me to call it out instantly the next time.

2. **Test the RAPP for accuracy** — Once named I can challenge the justification. Is this RAPP simply a reaction to prejudice, or is there rational justification? Is it accurate that all fat people are disgusting, self-absorbed, and irresponsible, or does reason suggest otherwise? The answer is no, they are not. I have had good friends and colleagues who are fat. In fact, I've been a little chubby myself at certain points throughout my life. So, no. My judgment is inaccurate and must be eliminated.

3. **Erase the RAPP** — If I establish that a RAPP is logically inaccurate (bad code), I must repair it or erase it, so that it doesn't continue loading and running automatically each time it is triggered. Because this RAPP defies logic (my brain does understand logic), I must instruct my brain that the "Fat-RAPP" is inaccurate, and it must stop repeating the story. You cannot get mad at yourself for continuing to run RAPPs that you have not deleted, that you have not instructed your brain to stop repeating. Since it is important to explicitly decode your brain, it helps to do a written exercise for this process, rather

than rely on the mental note, "Ditch the Fat RAPP and everything will be better," isn't good enough. You must issue the instruction to stop using it.

4. **Replace the RAPP** — To preempt the Fat-RAPP I substitute a new story that runs every time I see a fat person. The "Anti-Fat-RAPP." Some of the most important people I admire were fat at some point in their lives. "Churchill was fat." "Oprah is fat." "I am fat!" "Perhaps the person I am looking at is like me? Perhaps they are working on a cure for cancer."

5. **Abstraction RAPP** — The brain tends to abstract, rather than experience. It rushes to map sensory experiences from "instantaneous" into "symbols and sounds" so that it can classify and quantify them into memory, albeit a pale shadow of the real thing. Consider my compulsion to photograph (and post) almost every experience on Facebook — a digital extension of the brain's need to feed memory. Language and mathematics are the most common symbolisms used to represent reality, but there are other methods, too. Graphic art, music, and sculpture serve a similar function of capturing some essence or interpretation of truth. And generally, the more skilled the artist, the more of what is captured exceeds what is possible to represent through the spoken word. My brain expresses thoughts in words, and it is addicted to using them, whether or not the words are relevant to the reality being presented through the senses. It is a concept-analyzing abstracting machine that seeks sense from all it encounters. Sense is literally the chain of words it spontaneously creates in the effort to fold an experience into preexisting concepts it has formulated over the years.

The Certainty Principle tells us that these rivers of conceptualization can overwhelm our ability to accurately experience reality. So how do we stop it?

12.8 — The Brain-Jacking Defense

"... if you don't censor yourself, you end up with what you're most concerned about, but you haven't filtered it through your conscious mind. Then you craft it."
DAVID BYRNE

Brain-jacking is the brain's inclination for preempting my Mandate-related work by censoring intuition with prejudices and random fixations. The brain habitually rationalizes everything. Such chronic attention-shifting causes my productivity to flounder. Remediation begins with establish-

ing a defensive posture against the hijacking of my mandate. My warrior stance implies I am alert to the disposition of my brain, preventing it from hijacking my focus by intrusive and irrelevant thought. The metaphor is strong, but strength is the secret for a high-fidelity mandate. My Brain-jacking Alert System pinches, punches, or otherwise provokes me physically to interrupt the brain-jack once it begins. Even standing up and walking around the room or the block will often help restore focus on priorities. The solution is creating a personal alert system for signaling loss of focus, and then taking physical action to prevent it.

Drunken State of Uncertainty

The uncertainty state promoting brain-jacking is characterized the "3Fs." *F*atigue, *F*earfulness, and in*F*irmity, any of which compromise mental discipline, promoting a condition-centric state of mind. The result is akin to various degrees of drunkenness: At first a little goofy, followed by increasing levels of confusion, then surrendering to random, unmandated brain activity. My brain-jacking defense system requires me to establish personal routines that prevent the 3Fs from occurring. Creating a habit of deep sleep and periodic brain-rest by working in intervals, eliminates fatigue. Aerobic exercise relaxes the musculature, re-infusing brain and brawn with the chemistry required for high performance, proficiency, and avoidance of illness. Since what I consume dictates that chemistry, processed foods and excess carbohydrates are out. These constraints also promote fearlessness, but The Certainty Principle is itself a remedy for a fearful disposition.

Heart-Attack Smacked

Establishing a brain-jacking defense system, as with all disciplines, must be intimately subjective to be effective. I cannot effect changes in my operating system unless I am compelled to by a "heart attack" caliber cause. Change always fails when driven by vain imitation or a "grass is greener" motivation. "I want to be like him". Fact is, I change when I have no choice. I will impose the discipline to become a great golfer once I conclude that golf is fundamental to my Mandate.

12.9 — Forest for the Trees: Habituation

Habituation = My brain neglecting environmental factors that are constant (Thompson, 1966). In the same manner that a cat cannot see a mouse that is standing still, the brain ignores things it perceives as constants. But because human cognitive complexity is far greater than the cat's, the implications are exponentially greater than one more mouse in the house.

Optimizing bandwidth demands that the brain rapidly filter out anything that it deems as familiar or uninteresting (fades into the background). To the extent that my brain is trivially preoccupied, the domain of constancy expands to accommodate available processing, even to the point of absurdity.

Consider the phenomenon of losing my keys, which, it turns out, are lying conspicuously on the desk right in front of me. Or misplacing my glasses, which are comfortably perched on top of my head. Worse yet is ignoring my wife when my brain selects to disregard what she is saying as mundane in favor of listening to my own vanity driven thoughts such as, "My wife's comments are so mundane compared to my own pithy observations!"

The advantages of habituation are obvious. They provide me the capacity to laser focus on what my brain deems as the most important detail of the moment. Problems arise when my brain's choices of focus become distorted, habituating what is important, instead focusing on what is not. The implications are far-reaching, and can even lead to disaster. While driving a familiar route in my car, my vain brain may choose to attend to an incoming text message for a micro "I'm-important," dopamine rush, ignoring the obvious danger of such distraction.

12.10 — TCP, Churchill's Solitaire, and Karma

Churchill's Solitaire (CS) is a complex version of solitaire that Sir Winston played when in need of a relief from the relentless stress of wartime leadership. Compared with classic solitaire's win rate of two out of five, skilled CS players can expect one win every six to eight hands. CS's low win rate means

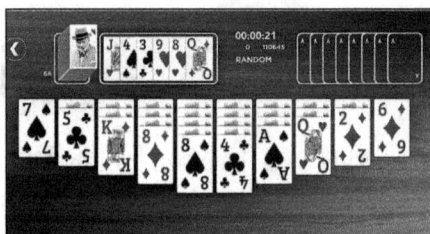

the time wasted pursuing losing hands is especially important to the overall strategy of racking up a high number of wins per hour of play, forcing decisions at the earliest possible juncture about which games are worth pursuing and which games are losers.

CS play is also unforgiving. When a player presumes a hand is winnable, progress relies on selecting the correct sequence of plays. Missing a single play virtually assures defeat.

The Certainty Principle is essentially about two things:

- optimizing attention to avoid games that cost me time, and
- missing plays that cost me the game.

> *"The best laid plans of mice and men often go awry."*
> BURNS, 1786

Outcomes are conditional, subject to external circumstances beyond my control. To optimize my mandate, I must learn to masterfully control those actions that are within my control.

CS is an effective exercise in learning to detach from outcomes, and focus instead on the quality of my choices. Emotional balance about the outcome of a given game enables a level of deep, unbiased, and situational analysis needed to distinguish a good from a poor play — a winning game from a losing game.

Generalizing the CS lesson, TCP helps neutralize personal enthrallment with a particular outcome, while providing the clarity to recognize when and how right actions need to be taken.

12.11 — Identity Rumination

What is good for a cow is not good for a human. Crudely speaking, a cow eats and swallows all it can while grazing, so that, at its leisure, it can vomit up and proceed with a fermentation process called rumination. A cow ruminates to hedge its nutritional requirements.

When the brain feasts in self, the regurgitant is Identity. The brain is a wanting machine, and in absence or even denial of a worthy problem or task its default primary want is identity. In boredom, it will seek out the most abstract reinforcement of self-image, often fringing on the absurd.

Again, *schadenfreude* is defined as deriving pleasure from the misfortune of others. What is the origin of such a response? The theory is based on the "at-least-it-didn't-happen-to-me" identity-reinforcing syndrome. My own identity, with respect to luck or judgment, is somehow validated by the failure or bad luck of another, even if there is no logical correlation, (consider "rubber-neckers" passing a car crash). Such righteousness is a common human emotive force wherein reason is co-opted by enthrallment with identity, even if it is logically indefensible. Identity politics is the phenomenon wherein adherents to one political viewpoint or candidate have so deeply ruminated it with self-image that disappointment manifests as anger, even violence. (Consider the election of Donald Trump.)

External validations of identity are doomed to disappoint because external conditions are always beyond the control of the individual. Outcomes are a crap shoot. Consistent reliance on external outcomes for definition of self leads to an emotional roller-coaster that triggers fear, regret, or worse. Though results do provide guidance or pointers for next action steps, if I wish to maintain a state of certainty, I must reject the tendency to identify personally with such outcomes.

To put a fine point on it, my purchase of a stock (regardless of the outcome) isn't a validation or demotion of me. It is only a validation of whether or not the cognitive process used to determine what and when to buy was accurate. And then it's still a crap-shoot!

Market dynamics are somewhat random (Pearson, 1905), being reliant on scores of variables invisible to the buyer. Even the finest quantitative analysis of a stock will result in a choice that delivers a random outcome that may or may not validate my decision. As such, identification with outcomes inevitably screw up my thinking, win or lose. While sustaining my confirmation bias that I am a genius, the elation of a win quickly passes. Identifying with a win leads to inflation of self, and distorts my future choices. Thanks to "identity rumination" the regrets associated with losing are enduring and demotivating. Disappointment can trigger a cascade of recollections of former failures, leading to paralysis.

A more mundane example of identity rumination is the desire to extract identity through association with material possessions. A nice wristwatch, a car, or a home are all material objects I may own, but they are not me. The brain tends to incorporate the ownership of such things into my identity through periodic regurgitation of such ownership to validate my importance. Such motives will always lead to disappointment because, in time, all material possessions succumb to habituation (the phenomenon of brain nominalization), if not physical decomposition. Even diamonds, beyond the novelty of newness, are not forever!

TCP reminds me of the importance of distinguishing between identification with a material possession, as opposed to valuing that material possession for the utility or aesthetic it provides. Buying a motorcycle for beauty of the design and the thrill of the experience of speeding around a tight corner is not the same as buying it so I can wear the T-shirt. Owning artwork for the powerful emotional impact I experience with each viewing isn't the same as owning it to impress my guests, or for its investment value.

If it's the latter I am bound to be disappointed when I eventually learn that my appeal to others is based on my things or my wealth, and not on me.

Here are some examples of how the brain ruminates to fatten identity.

Behavior	Emotive force	Example
Hubris	arrogance	childish lack of deference
Judgementalism	righteousness	chronic prejudice
Materialism	greed	selfishness
Victimism	despair	blaming others
Schadenfreude	apathy	lacking empathy for others
Haste	regret	lacking presence of mind
Abusiveness	dominance	demeaning others
Religiosity	righteousness	holier-than-thou attitude
Subservience	humiliation	chronic self-deprecation
Conformity	fear	chronic need to be part of a herd

And many, many more.

12.12 — Brain Games

So far, The Certainty Principle gives my brain a pretty bad rap. But my brain is not the enemy. My brain is the tool I use to play the game of manifesting my mandate, while considering external conditions.

Robert Nash won the Nobel Prize for his Theory on Games.

$$Pi(t) >/= 1 - Pj(t+1) ==> Pi(t) + Pj(t+1) >/= 1.$$
NASH, JR., 1950

Game theorists use the Nash Equilibrium to analyze the outcome of the strategic interaction of opposing decision makers.

In TCP terms, the formula provides a way of predicting the most likely outcomes when my choice is reliant on the decisions of the others.

The simple insight underlying Nash's idea is that my predictions are more accurate when I ask what my opponent might do, taking into account my opponent's decision-making strategy.

The importance to TCP is that vanity promotes myopic decision-making. It tends to exclude reasonable consideration of opposing factors, thus demoting cooperation. The smart choice (decision) about my next play comes down to the sum of the probabilities of me (player "1") winning at time t, plus the probability of me losing to an opponent on the next move (t+1) (here the aggregate of external forces). Generally, my wisest choice of action (called equilibrium) is not what is best for me alone. Rather the best choice is one that would result in the most reasonable gain or least loss for both/all parties. My best outcome in playing a game is to use my brain to decipher the least risk course of play for all parties, because that is the most probable outcome.

This may sound obvious, but obvious does not always mean operational. Gaming the brain for achievement requires us to evaluate the likelihood of our strategy winning versus the likelihood of our opponent losing.

In TCP, the opponent is the conditional environment, the aggregate chance that manifesting my expected outcomes will not prevail. If one were playing Blackjack, the likelihood of winning on the next turn of a card — prompting us to raise our bet — is the sum of the probabilities of me getting a winning card dealt versus the likelihood of the dealer being dealt a losing card. I rationally play based on the combination of these two factors.

Certainty exists when my brain is sufficiently alert to reason clearly about both internal and external likelihoods of the games I play. Game play is necessary for me to advance my mandate, and equilibrium is the most likely path to progress. Like a sailboat tacking, the wind that advances me is the unabstracted reality, and to keep advancing I must keep my brain very close to that wind, unencumbered by the anchor of identity.

12.13 — Velcro™

The psychosis of identity-seeking causes my brain to "cling" to any fabric of experience that reinforces the epic story of myself. This "Velcro Effect" (TVE) increases the friction of my daily decision-making. Self-seeking stories are like the little hooks of the hook-and-loop system that makes Velcro so effective for attaching things. The thousands of identity-driven stories cataloged on its neurological hard drive are like the little hooks grabbing each scintilla of data that it can construe as self-validating. If my stories provide the hooks, my judgments

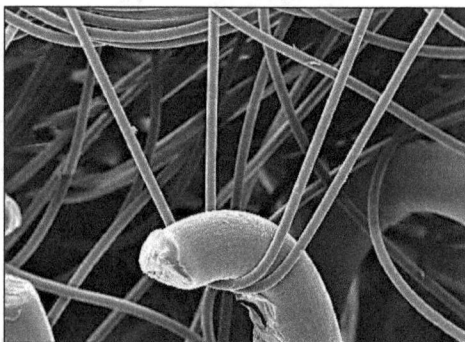

are the loops. TVE results from my identity-confirmation-bias seeking external data that it can easily judge, right or wrong, to keep me in the right!

The comedian George Carlin highlighted this phenomenon in his classic story about driving on the freeway in Los Angeles.

"Anyone who drives slower than me is an idiot, and anyone who drives faster than me is a maniac!"
GEORGE CARLIN

What Carlin leaves out is how fast he drives because it doesn't matter. TVE compels him to judge others behavior in a way that is self-validating — he is the gold standard!

Identity-driven confirmation encumbers because it puts a bias algorithm in between experience and reasoning. Not surprisingly, TVE leads to the sensation of being stuck. As my identity seeks to attach itself for meaning I can become indecisive and confused over even the simplest of decisions. In time, TVE diminishes capacity, as my brain accumulates mountains of self-validating data stuck all over it. Unchallenged, TVE eventually burdens its host to the point of self-destruction. Absurd behaviors, such as rejection of the beneficial and embracing of the harmful, alert me that my judgment has become distorted by such attachments.

In my alcoholic period, I selectively sought any story that validated that my identity as a drinker. I ignored my first-hand experience with alcohol shredding my father's life in favor of identifying with legendary drinking habits of Alexander the Great! Whether my identity-epic is self-aggrandizing or self-deprecating, TVE eventually destroys its host, while driving away those around them.

Fortunately, the emotional sensation of being "stuck in a moment" is an early warning of TVE. If I find myself cursing a driver who cut me off hours ago, I'm stuck. If a disagreement with a colleague stalks my brain for days on end, I'm stuck. If I am haunted by a parental insult from childhood, I'm really stuck. TCP provides the awareness to respond when my "stuck signal" my tells me I'm getting "Velcro-ed" to an experience by my identity.

The Certainty Principle replaces Velcro with Teflon™ by demoting Outcome-Identity-infused thinking (OI) with Horizon-Mandate (HM) centricity. I say Teflon because my brain can't stick to experiences that don't matter much. When my mission and the time-frame is large enough, most problems appear trivial or, at most, temporary. As it was with Magellan, TCP's grand scope of accountability frees me to evaluate obstacles and solutions realistically, less all the emotional attachment to my stories in my head.

12.14 — Intuition

Intuition (according to Wikipedia) is having a "nose" for knowledge without proof, evidence, or conscious reasoning, or without understanding how the knowledge was acquired. It is choice without thought. Identity blocks intuition in the same manner that processed foods block digestion.

To the extent that my RAPPs define my experience, I am insulated from real experience, and my capacity for making reality-based choices, intuitively, is limited.

Intuition is key to certainty. Learning to trust intuition leads to insights that are impossible through cognitive milling alone. Certainty is achieved by learning to rely on intuition through the non-rational, non-binary, identity-free skill of seeing things as they really are. And this path can deliver extraordinary insights.

> *"The intuitive mind is a sacred gift and the rational mind is a faithful servant... it is intuition that holds the power to save you."*
> EINSTEIN

If brain function is like digestion, intuition is like breathing. Most thoughts are the transient by-products of the abstracting device called the brain in its persistent course of rationalizing sensory input. Let's call this "braining." If braining becomes my default state, I am susceptible to the illusion that my brain's thought domain is the limitation of what is possible and understandable, or even the entire domain of fact. After all, if I should become enthralled with the impossible task of labeling and judging (in terms of how it defines me) every piece of data that enters my senses, how long before I come to believe my braining as reality? Not long! Once I recognize that identity is a complete fabrication — an illusion — I begin seeing things as they really are. Remember, the brain is only efficient as a linear, single-port, bi-directional processor. It is easily overpowered by my compulsion with identity.

Like many around the age of 16 — about the same time I became preoccupied with girls — I was having a crisis of identity. My self-image had degraded to the point that I was near suicidal (typical kid from a broken home, aimlessly reliant on the charity of my friends). This process had taken a few years, but for a self-consumed kid like me the confusion around fitting in had finally become intolerable.

One cool Sunday night in October, a friend's parents had dropped me off to catch the last train back to my hometown. I was too embarrassed to tell them I didn't have the money for a ticket. As the last train pulled out of the station, I realized I was really stuck. I had nothing but the clothes on my back, which included a sweater and an old Navy-issue, wool P-coat, plus a small backpack with a sweater and a beat-up empty wallet holding a picture of my father and a four-leafed clover he'd given me, plus a picture of my sister Dee. I put on the sweater and sat down on a bench. I was stuck. I had no choice but to come to terms with being alone, cold, broke, hungry, and miles from a warm bed. I bundled up and slid into the dark end of the station so I wouldn't be seen.

As usual, my brain began grinding away about how miserable I was — how much I wanted to eat, be warm, and be with my friends. But this loop had been running in my brain for a few years, and I was becoming sick and tired of hearing it. I was ready to do anything to end it, once and for all. I was bored with going over the same needy ground again and again. I was bored with myself.

As I gazed up at the stars it occurred to me that maybe my constant wanting (bitching, really) was part of my problem. Maybe detaching from all the stuff that I constantly craved would provide me some peace. Even then, it seemed illogical.

All I needed — warmth, food, and companionship — seemed perfectly natural. But the powerful intuition — that wanting was making me suffer — felt right, even if the wanting seemed justified.

During the 20 or 30 minutes of sitting there in the cold, my eyes remained fixed on the night sky. I'd been focusing so hard on one cluster of stars that I barely blinked. I was suddenly rattled back to reality by the uncanny sensation of being physically drawn away — a strong sensation of letting go, like dropping rapidly in an elevator. Breaking my gaze, I regained composure, and reminded myself about my insight about "wanting."

Within minutes the appeal of the "letting go" sensation drew my eyes back to the star. I was scared, but curious about this current running through my brain and body. I didn't know if I was slipping into insanity, or out of consciousness. After a few rounds, I realized that I was unwittingly preparing to surrender entirely to the uncanny gravity. That's when the thought occurred to me, "What if there's no coming back?"

I reasoned I needed a safety switch, so I set a rule my head that I would return to the bench if I reached the point that I no longer cared if I ever returned to the bench again. This decision infused the experience with a new sense of confidence. For the first time I knew I had overcome, or at least completely neutralized, fear by controlling my thoughts. That control allowed me to free myself from caring about what was next. Whatever awaited me was what awaited me. I was prepared for anything, good or bad, that followed.

"I'll go back when I don't care if I ever go back again" was the affirmation I repeated over and over, hundreds of times. I don't know where that thought came from, but each time I repeated it I could feel the tug of my brain holding me back.

But each time I felt myself moving farther and farther away from the bench. My attachment to, and desire for, the familiar — all who I knew and cared for — became weaker and weaker. Part of me was afraid. But a larger part wanted to go. So, I kept repeating, "I'll go back when I don't care if I ever go back again," until the instant when the connection snapped, and I was free.

The next thing I knew, a train was pulling into the station (turns out, there was another train). Now cold and hungry, I sprinted to get aboard. Whether they threw me off at the next station, I didn't care — I was freezing. But when I opened the door into the bright, toasty car I realized something had changed.

I'd come to associate riding trains, especially at night, as a sad, even lonely, experience. Many weekends I'd taken the train from one friend's house to another, feeling kind of lost. But not this time. As I entered the nearly empty car there was no longer that familiar feeling of self-pity. In its place was the unfamiliar, disturbing sensation that I was exactly where I was supposed to be.

To be as accurate as I can in words, nothing looked unfamiliar, but the feeling I had was radically unfamiliar. I would not have been the least bit surprised if the conductor had walked up and told me I was dead. Instead, he asked for my ticket. After explaining that I had no money he asked where I was going, punched out a receipt and told me not to let it happen again.

My identity, which constantly filtered and colored every inch of experience, was gone. Clarity was all that remained. Unadorned, unjustified clarity.

On the ride home alone that night in the train car I was awed — and frightened — by the imposing sense of reality that accompanied every turn of my head. I knew the experience was mine, entirely individual. But it was so foreign that I was convinced I was "losing it." In retrospect, I've likened it to anxiety that an inmate might feel when finally set free after a long confinement. Though I knew it was real, and I was stronger for it, I was unprepared for the impact of seeing things as they really are.

For months afterwards I tried erasing all memory of the experience, writing it off to teenage angst, even though I knew in my heart otherwise. I sought safe harbor back in my identity and its familiar self-talk, to which I attribute many poor choices and missed opportunities. The familiar misery of vanity might have masked the certainty I'd achieved at 16, but it was always there below the surface. And not long after that, I threw on a backpack and watch cap, stuck out my thumb, and I was gone.

12.15 — Declaration of Certainty

"A man with outward courage dares to die; a man with inner courage dares to live."
TZU, TAO TE CHING, 4TH CENTURY BC

Like electricity, Certainty scared and fascinated me. After years of delusional self-talk, I got zapped, grounded, and energized. But again, it scared me. What I knew for sure was: a.) The core of what makes me, me (hard to define in words) in reality is permanent, as in forever, and b.) What I formerly thought was me (my identity) was an illusion. Pure vapor.

This knowing followed me around like a disciplinary instructor. My fear of it caused me to ignore it, but the knowing was never far away, standing by, waiting to strike when my brain became too foolish and self-absorbed.

My only reprieve was fresh experience. A cross-country hitchhike, building a cabin, trekking in India, or climbing a slippery cliff, all commanded my absolute attention, and spared me the switch. Otherwise, I was alone under the wheel of Certainty. At Berkeley I learned that physics was about discovering the factors and functions of forever. It was the first time I felt there were others who were like-minded. I was inspired, but I lacked the language skills (higher mathematics) of my new fraternity. So, as the concepts became more challenging, I found myself isolated again.

It took years to connect the dots, years before I understood that with each difficult episode, I was gaining greater courage to confront the timeless accountability I'd discovered at 16.

I'd been unfair to myself, beating myself up over denial of the freedom of the long view. People living under tyrannical governments submit to the tyranny until things get bad enough. That's when they commit to action. How long would I live under the tyranny of my brain's temporal identity before giving myself permission to declare a preference for something superior?

Forever is better. Forever is a better home for me than what my mundane, temporal brain could possibly provide. I needed its logic to play the reasoning games, resolving the problems and tasks presented to me. But logic was not enough. Certainty was the universal solvent rendering all of life's obstacles into their proper priority. Once I gave myself permission to embrace Certainty, everything began to change.

But permission is not enough to perpetuate Certainty. When I'm not problem-solving, my brain gets bored and mischievously turns its cognitive powers to self-gratification. This adolescent tendency interferes with clear reasoning by identity-feeding an internal dialog. "He's a jerk because . . ." "She's an idiot because . . ." "I'm a genius!"

Certainty requires courage, but such cognition is a substitute for courage. By adulthood, these identity games become highly developed — so deeply habituated that they dominate experience. Certainty signals us when the Identity Game threatens to consume us.

√	"I'm stuck": When I attach identity to future outcomes.
√	"I'm afraid": When I feel I'm losing my identity.
√	"I'm angry": When my identity is attachment to a concept.
√	"I regret": When my identity is attached to past outcomes.
√	"I'm selfish": When I attach my identity to things.
√	"I'm important": When my identity is attached to judging others.
√	"I'm in despair": When my identity is attached to comparing myself to others.
√	"I'm frustrated": When I identify with a particular outcome.
√	"I need to survive": No, I don't, and I can't.
√	"Righteousness": When my identity is attached to a position.

Many signals point to Certainty. But the underlying source of the pointers is always my brain's preoccupation with validating its own story as unique, separate, and righteous. When the organ I rely on to digest data and problem-solve becomes preoccupied with vanity, uncertainty grows.

Learning to heed such pointers first requires that I learn to pay attention. Certainty is the vigilance to perceive and dismiss the frivolous vanity games my brain conjures up for me, rather than allowing them to take over. Screaming at the driver in front of me in a traffic jam, anger over the comments of a political rival, or beating myself up for one failure or another, are all uncertainty creating reactions that point out that my brain isn't presenting things the way they really are. But developing the skill of vigilance is only possible once I decide I need it. If I'm happier in the vanity illusion, I will never attain Certainty.

> *Cypher: "You know, I know this steak doesn't exist.*
> *I know that when I put it in my mouth, the Matrix is telling my brain that it is juicy and delicious.*
> *After nine years, you know what I realize?*
> *Ignorance is bliss."*
> THE MATRIX, WACHOWSKI & WACHOWSKI, 1999

Cypher chooses the illusion of The Matrix, and makes important, unethical decisions to preserve the illusion.

To preserve vanity, I must decide that my identity is bigger than my mandate, and that outcomes are more important that the long-term accountability for my decisions. The value of Certainty is the same value of being finally, comfortably at home. Freedom from the influences of judging and being judged, and labeling and being labeled.

Absent uncertainty, everything occurs about as it should. Everyone fulfills their role about as I would expect. This is because Certainty is true home, the internal domain where I am 100 percent in control. It is always there waiting for me when the game is over.

Knowing true home always brings me back in harmony, despite the silliness of my brain's games. But staying certain is hard when there is so much profit in feeding my brain's insatiable synthesis of identity. NΩ

Chapter 13
Burning Uncertainty ——

13.1 — Torching the Talking Heads

The News Media is a "pusher," paid to deliver the eyeballs of uncertainty junkies. Eyeballs are attracted to media that is coherent with the threads of fear and regret the uncertain brain constantly traces and retraces. Most popular media formulate content to cultivate the vanities of the spectators watching it.

I am fascinated with death, destruction, pestilence, deprivation, and fall of man because it reinforces my own, albeit miserable, self-righteousness. "If it bleeds, it leads" is the morbid editorial principle underpinning much popular news and TV programming, simply because identity reinforcement, regardless of how cynical it is delivers ad revenues, and the media "suits" gladly twist the knife to serve that end.

Barely one week after the tragic death of Kobe Bryant, his daughter, and seven others in a helicopter crash, Gayle King on CBS, interviewing the WNBA's Lisa Leslie (Trepany, 2020), asked about Bryant's reputation as a philanderer. Blaming her employer/network for the question is illustrative of media's arrogance when it comes to leveraging vanity to drive eyeballs. The hyper-competition compels irresponsibility, even if it means disparaging the recently dead.

If you want to know the most common uncertainty denominator of a specific demographic group, examine the media they invite to consistently prey on them. The more eyeballs attracted, the more primordial the motive.

The fall of man has instinctive appeal to my identity. Addiction to news media that sensationalizes — even fabricates — tragedy does so because it will appeal to spectator's vanity. The sadomasochistic inclination of extracting pleasure in observation of someone else's suffering ("at-least-it-wasn't-me") is an example of such validation. If I was spared, I am favored, and, therefore, special. If I am not spared, I am the victim, and, therefore, special. Either way I win! But I wouldn't know I'd won without the media pumping the non-stop, hot-pink slime of "If it bleeds, it leads" into my brain. Modern media delivers a boot, spike, pop, or slam (insert your junkie term of choice) of self-righteousness vanity directly on demand from our cell phones.

Stopping it is akin to quitting nicotine — nearly impossible. Impossible, that is, as long as my reliance on external validation, programmed since birth, remains unbroken. The only escape I have found to be reliable in severing (and I mean cutting off) that "specialness instinct" is embracing The Certainty Principle as my reality. There is something in the "forever horizon" that relieves me of the need to emotionally validate my significance. I repeat, this is not about religion, faith, or dogma. TCP is releasing into the initially disorienting, yet finally and obviously accurate, brain domain, where vanity-fed identity is an illusion. Once achieved, the need to feed identity once and for all (thank God) begins to fade.

13.2 — Burning My Résumé

Few documents codify my identity more than my résumé. The extremities to which I will habitually conflate and fabricate my importance for the purpose of vanity is boundless. I am unscrupulous about embellishing my story to appear smarter, more accomplished, and more attractive to gain advantages over others. Nothing evidences this lack of objectivity better than my résumé.

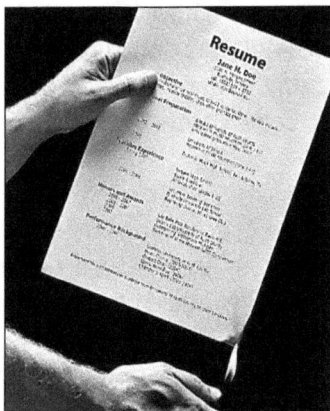

Time to burn it. Making it this far in the TCP story deserves memorialization by little ceremony. So print out a copy of your résumé or CV, take it out in the back yard and light it up. Why? Because nothing enthralls identity more than the intense effort I put into writing and polishing my résumé, fixating my brain on the notion that my value as a human being is the chronology of past outcomes, both factual and embellished, and listed on a couple of sheets of 8"x11" Southworth™ linen paper. How can I remain dispassionate about the highly conditional endeavor of job seeking, particularly if I am ignorant of the selection algorithm of the Applicant Tracking System used to evaluate my résumé?

Résumés are not in and of themselves the problem. But my brain's compulsion for inflating identity is — in two important ways. When I am job hunting, I come to see my comprehensive and intimate value as an individual in what's described in my paperwork. Therefore, when my résumé is conditionally rejected, my value is rejected — an illogical, but perfectly natural, identity-first response with a depressive effect. There are myriad reasons a résumé is rejected, and most of them have little or nothing to do with the writer.

There is the custom of making résumés rearward looking, and that creates a multitude of problems. One is that self-hind-sight is seldom 20/20, and the tendency to inflate or obscure the past is powerful. CareerBuilder reports that 58 percent of employees have been caught in a lie on their résumé. (Tarpey, 2014). That's only those who get caught! Not necessarily damaging in and of itself, unless the writer pathologically comes to believe their own fabrications.

Consider the Sen. Elizabeth Warren case, where ambitions drove her to fabricate a Native American heritage that she willingly perpetuated throughout her career until it was finally debunked by DNA testing.

Focusing on the past has other risks, such as the tendency to get stuck there. The more I identify with the past, the more inertia to future action. The future is fresh, but the past is stale and can even become toxic when it dominates identity. The opposite is also true. The more forward looking I am, the freer I am to take necessary actions. Leonardo di ser Piero da Vinci's famous letter to the Duke of Milan provides evidence in the power of this forward perspective (Cenedella, 2016), for which Leonardo was richly rewarded. Da Vinci's résumé begins nearly every paragraph with "I will . . .," or "I can . . ." There seems to be a complete lack of retrospect, as if da Vinci understood that all statements about past achievements read as sentimental and dubious.

More than ever, my résumé is first and foremost a game piece in the digital winnowing of a stack of such documents, so understanding the program is a priority. That said, regardless of how you must formulate the résumé to play the game effectively, never lose track of the truth — da Vinci's 500-year-old message is timeless wisdom.

My value is not what I did, and where I come from. It is my talent and skill, and where I am going with them and what I will create. Leonardo's grand perspective on his fundamental worth is the key to why I and many others are still writing about him 500 years after his death.

13.3 — Vanity Sinks the *Titanic*

"Even God himself couldn't sink this ship…"
ATTRIBUTED TO CAPTAIN SMITH
BY SURVIVOR L. BEESLET, BEESLEY, 1912

"Cognitive distortion" is how psychologists refer to the tendency to complete a scenario with our own preconceived conclusions, particularly when the scenario seems familiar, or when we fear the reality. At worst, we filter and distort the data to our liking to preserve our identity's attachment to being right.

This is the "Capt. Smith" syndrome — an allusion to the captain of *RMS Titanic* who was famously quoted saying, "I cannot imagine any condition which would cause this ship to founder." Approaching midnight on April 14, 1911, cognitive

distortion prevented Smith from seeing what had become clear to his subordinates, including Thomas Andrews, the chief designer. The ship was sinking.

At 4:00 am, the first rescue ship, *RMS Carpathia* under Captain Arthur H. Ronstron, arrived on the disaster scene. Ronstron had responded immediately to the SOS (referred to as "CDQ" in 1911), steaming 58 miles at top speed in an iceberg field from the point where he received the distress call from the *RMS Titanic* foundering four hours to his northwest. Though initially he was unable to confirm the message, he commanded an immediate emergency response, pivoting his ship, jettisoning cargo, and racing in the direction of the distress call. Ronstron's action exemplified undistorted decision-making. The more comfortable supposition of a possible false alarm did not outweigh the immense consequences of being wrong. Sadly, *Carpathia*'s distance proved too great to spare the lives of hundreds of passengers in the frigid waters of the North Atlantic. Especially tragic was that another vessel, the *SS Californian*, much closer to *Titanic*, was commanded by a captain who lacked Ronstron's undistorted clarity of command.

At 8:30 am (4.5 hours after the *Carpathia* had arrived) the *SS Californian*, under Capt. Stanley Lord, arrived after traveling just 20 miles. Soon after *Titanic* struck the iceberg, Lord was notified by crew on watch of visual cues that *Titanic*, less than an hour's run to their south, was in trouble. Court transcripts chronicle a tragic failure of communications and executive decision-making. The *Californian* crew's keen awareness of the dangerous ice field surrounding both ships (California had stopped dead in the water until daybreak to better navigate the field) failed to alert them to the possible implications of what they were seeing with their own eyes. The stunning failure of logic and leadership compounded when both subordinates on watch reported *Titanic*'s odd list to the starboard bow against the waterline, paling deck lights, and emergency flares (mistaken as celebratory skyrockets) seven hours before. Upon the report, Capt. Lord returned to his bed. His desperate day-break race to the wreck was far too late. While Lord slept within view of her, *Titanic* went to the bottom 12,000 feet below her, taking 1,490 souls with her.

Fearing an ice collision in the darkness, Lord had stopped the *Californian*, waiting for daybreak to proceed. In an ironic twist, just minutes before hitting the iceberg *Titanic's* radio operator had blocked repeated warnings from *Californian* alerting *Titanic* to the escalating danger. The great ship continued speeding into the murky ice field at 23 knots, far too fast to stop or avoid collision. Though the captain and crew of the *Californian* were keenly aware of the danger, they failed to respond when confronted with evidence that the very fate they feared most was visited upon *Titanic*.

Do I tend to make decisions in defense of my own preconceived, even stated, positions? Or am I sufficiently unattached from such identity-reinforcing thinking that I can see the path forward clearly and accurately?

There was a broadly held misperception at the time — stated by Capt. Smith prior to the disaster, and Lord later in his court testimony — that *Titanic* was indestructible. Did Smith identify so powerfully with his public commitment to this delusion (clearly, not an engineering reality) that it disabled his ability to reason, and ignore the dangers? If so, was it vanity that sank *Titanic*? We will never know. Capt. Smith went down with the ship. Furthermore, was it identity that prevented Lord from responding in a timely manner?

The remarkable exchange below, from the American inquiry of the disaster, implicated Lord and his first officer George F. Stewart in a cover-up of their negligent response to events of April 14, 1912, on board the *Californian*. (Commission, 1912)

Now [First Officer George F. Steward], I should like to follow this. As far as your memory serves you, did you enter into that logbook everything that you found on the scrap log sheet?

Yes.

You observe there is nothing at all in your logbook about seeing distress signals?

Yes.

Is there anything?

No, nothing.

Nothing at all?

No.

No reference to any of these events of the night (of the sinking) at all?

No.

(The Commissioner.) *Does that convey to you that there was no reference to those events in the scrap log?*

Yes, my Lord.

(The Solicitor-General.) *Give us your views. Supposing you were keeping the scrap log on a watch when you were in ice, and supposing you saw a few miles to the southward a ship sending up what appeared to you to be distress signals, would not you enter that in the log?*

Yes - I do not know.

(The Commissioner.) *Oh, yes you do?*

Yes, I daresay I should have entered it, but it was not in our scrap logbook.

(The Solicitor-General.) *That is not what I asked you. What I asked you was — apply your mind to it — supposing you had been keeping the scrap log in those circumstances and you saw*

*distress signals being sent up by a ship a few miles from you,
is that, or is not that, a thing you would enter in the log?*
Yes.

(The Commissioner.) *How do you account for it not being
there?*
I do not know, my Lord.

It was careless not to put it in, was it not?
Or forgetful.

*Forgetful? Do you think that a careful man is likely to forget
the fact that distress signals have been going on from a neigh-
boring steamer?*
No, my Lord.

(The Commissioner) *Then do not talk to me about forgetfulness.*

(The Solicitor-General.) *The scrap logbook is intended to be
kept at the time, is it not, as the things happen?*
**Yes, Sir, but they generally
write them up at the end of
the watch.**

And you were there at 4 o'clock at the end of the watch?
Yes.

*And Mr. Stone told you then at 4 o'clock that he had seen these
signals?*
Yes.

(The Commissioner.) *And they had been sending messages to
the Captain about them?*
Yes.

(The Solicitor-General.) *Three times?*
Yes.

The frequency of those occasions when I explicitly conform the facts into lies, as above, in hopes of preserving my external identity pales in comparison with the countless internal reality modifications my brain continuously makes to justify my vanity. I may choose to buy a fancy car or clothing, even if I can't afford such, in the effort to appear successful. But such delusions are relatively benign compared to the habit of inflating my own self-worth through the internal dialog of comparing and judging of others.

One might say that attachment to such repetitive self-delusion is, after all, only human. Moss is literally attached to the northern sides of trees and rocks. Squirrels are attached to acorns. Moths are attached to bright light. Eagles are attached to soaring. Elephants are attached to squirting water out of their trunks. These all-natural attachments are related to physical survival. Only humans attach to processes centered on survival of self, survival of identity, and, as such, can become a preponderant "doing" of human life.

Addiction suggests an attachment to a "doing" that degrades the doer. Because the brain has difficultly distinguishing reality from repetitive thought, such self-thoughts create a virtual reality that becomes difficult to distinguish from the real thing. Because human endeavor brings challenges, such repetitive thoughts tend to comply with confirmation bias that is self-affirming. After all, why would I possibly lend credence to a point of view that is antithetical to my stated position (the Capt. Smith Syndrome). When I allow either self-deprecating or self-aggrandizing stories, fixed in memory, to be triggered and reinforced by a distorted interpretation of real events, I am feeding my addiction to identity.

> *"People generally see what they look for*
> *and hear what they listen for."*
> LEE, 1960

The opposite of identity-attachment is self-indifference. Self-indifference is developing a skill for ignoring my brain's compulsion to reactively fit reality into my vanity framework and narrative. Indifference to my recurrent and familiar thought patterns and behaviors is superior to attachment, because, regardless of their nature, such attachments obscure and erode the clarity of experience. Indifference is not rejection, After all, occasionally even a repeated thought is accurate. But indifference removes the "wanting." Removing want liberates the brain to process in real time, freeing up the machinery of imagination and innovation.

Captain Lord of the *SS Californian* chose attachment over self-indifference when he encountered data that suggested that a steamer (*RMS Titanic*) was in trouble. Though clearly visible, Capt. Lord chose to interpret the reality of the emergency flares in terms of what was personally comfortable — a celebration — rather than confront the reality that the listing ship was foundering. At 58 miles, Captain Rostron of *Carpathia* was indifferent to his brain's more self-comforting responses to *Titanic*'s SOS, pivoting 180 degrees and speeding to the scene while casting cargo overboard to make room for survivors. The contrast in those choices of action had historic consequences. The results? *Carpathia* collected 712 survivors, *Californian*, 0.

Developing a skill for self-indifference influences choices of action that have important implications. The more significant the choice of action, the more naturally adherent my attachment is to the patterns that are familiar to me and, therefore, the more distorted my reasoning. And this can become chronic. Neurotic obesity stems from compulsive eating to find insulation from the reality of difficult choices. Or it can even take the place of making such choices altogether. The cycle is self-reinforcing to the extent that even insignificant choices quickly escalate to the level of triggering, the "Too hard, time to eat a pie" response.

When attachment becomes chronic, often the solution is to dull the senses to insulate myself from reality. One in six American adults (17 percent) were prescribed psychiatric drugs in 2016, and 13 percent of American adults report regular illicit drug use. About half are regular alcohol consumers (weekly). More than seven million children under the age of 17 were prescribed psychiatric drugs in 2017. NΩ

CHAPTER 14
——— TCP LIMITING CHOICES ———

Randomness does not perpetuate life. Sustainable patterns of behavior do. A mouse is a mouse because of its habitual survival activities, which have evolved over time — not by choice, but by the pressures of natural selection. If life itself is a pattern of action, then the most highly evolved state is man. Modern man is a unique life form that evolves mainly by choice.

> *"With all of these forks in the roads of our path*
> *why do so many choose to take the knife."*
> LICCIONE, 2012

The trait that distinguishes humans is our capacity for choosing which patterns to implement and which to abandon. Only humans willfully alter patterns of behavior to suit chosen horizons of achievement.

Important to recognize here is that all choices are not equal. Much of modern choice is merely consumerism marketed to feel meaningful. I can go grocery shopping and feel a sense of achievement based on the sheer volume of choices I am forced to make in the course of getting from one end of the store to the other. Meaningful decisions are different — they change my trajectory. The willpower to remove an old behavior, and diligently practice replacing it with a better aligned pattern of behavior, is the definitive skill at the highest strata of human achievement. All human endeavors were achieved by people who mastered the competency for disciplining their brain to alter their own behavior patterns, and influence the behaviors of others, even if ever so slightly.

> *"The reality distortion field was a confounding mélange of a charismatic rhetorical style, an indomitable will, and an eagerness to bend any fact to fit the purpose at hand. Amazingly, the reality distortion field seemed to be effective, even if you were acutely aware of it, although the effects would fade after Steve (Jobs) departed. We would often discuss potential techniques for grounding it ... but after a while most of us gave up, accepting it as a force of nature."*
> HERTZFEILD, 1981

If there is a skill most valuable to me, it is this one: The combination of even a modest, but well-embedded horizon, and a tireless will to align behaviors and actions with that horizon, delivers magnificent, even miraculous outcomes.

14.1 — Practice

The practice of Certainty is, well, practice! The mind of a true genius might retain everything it learns the first time, but

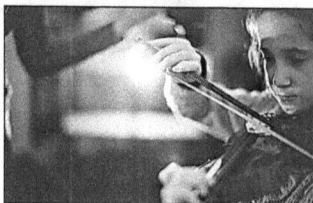

personally, I need to rehearse and rehearse and rehearse to get it right.

In 2010, I signed up for a terrific sales executive program to improve my skills for getting deals done. The materials, the training, and the coaching were all high quality. Even with constant repetition of the material, I required coaching and periodic training to remain competent in my deal making skills.

If specific skills are necessary for the efficient and effective execution of my work — for delivering on my mandate — I must get regularly scheduled practice and coaching to upgrade that expertise. Failing this diligence will degrade progress on my mandate.

I was enrolled in a first-class theater program during my high school years. My instructor, Cindy Louden, drew equity-caliber performances out of her students, mainly through the power of her diligent (and multiple!) rehearsals. She would drill us on recall, character, voice, blocking, and stage-presence until we could perform our plays in our sleep. As evidence, her practices so deeply rooted dialog in my brain that decades later I still have nightmares about forgetting lines during one of her performances!

Same routines deliver same results. It is impossible for me to advance intellectually or materially from the status quo without changing my brain's programming. But how do I do it? We've said that the brain lacks the systemic adaptability of even the simplest computer. For example, I cannot delete brain files. Rigorous rehearsal and the will to change is what separates the people who do new things from the people who just dream about doing new things.

14.2 — The Practice of Certainty

If alignment of actions with my mandate is key to supremacy, then what of The Certainty Principle? Wherein lies the value and the implementation of all the rest of it?

TCP is an operating principle, which is to say it is not a horizon in and of itself, but rather the source code upon which all other alignments are carried out. The key to TCP adoption is first accepting the fact that examining one's mental habitudes is a priority. Will an entrenched alcoholic consider sobriety? Is a religious zealot willing to examine her existence secularly?

Is an identity-bound leftist open to investigating the roots of conservative ideology objectively? The impediments to transformational thinking always find root cause in the TCP third factor: Identity. All struggles to improve, to elevate, to seek greater horizons are weighted down by the massive anchor of Identity. So, integration of TCP itself is encumbered by a component of TCP, to paraphrase Shakespeare:

"First, kill vanity."

14.3 — Losing Myself: The Ubiquity of You

The experience of "losing oneself" often results when the environment is so foreign or the interaction is so intense that the enthrallment with self-definition surrenders to a larger, deeper experience. Entering an ancient and magnificent cathedral can leave me so awestruck that the sense of individual identity is lost to an expansive sense of wonder at the overwhelming beauty and history of the place. Similarly, hearing a live orchestra play Beethoven's Sixth Symphony carries my experience of the moment into a larger domain that includes the composer himself and the generations moved by the sheer beauty of the composition. Though not religiously inclined, I once stood for hours before the original of Bernardino Luini's "Madonna and Child," tears streaming down my face. It seemed I'd surrendered to the centuries of those before me who also felt the passion captured forever by the artist who so lovingly created it. Most anyone visiting Yosemite National Park for the first time is so moved by the grandeur of the place as to be struck speechless — in its own way, a natural "spiritual" experience.

Such departures from identity into an intense reality experience are important touchstones to the freedom of feeling completely embedded in the manifesting moment — the smallness of being the same with all material things.

Why is such experience important to TCP? For the same reason that walks in nature are important. In these mute moments we are imbued with the reality of being part of something much larger than ourselves. In our day-to-day, identity-filled lives, it is easy to become enthralled with ourselves as the center of the universe. But this is not reality. Physically we are made up of the same fundamental particles as everything spinning around us. As such, in a physical sense, it is impossible for me to separate myself from the physical reality within which I exist. In the base reality as we know it to be, we are absolutely the same as the material world within which we exist. Such a fact is not a revelation to anyone who passed high school physics. But my brain creates such a habitude of individuality that it becomes nearly impossible to experience myself as part of the natural whole. I am in effect, everywhere. And as such, the absurdity of an individual identity becomes very apparent. It's the simple examination of the basic science of reality — at least reality as we perceived it through our five senses.

14.4 — Manifesting My Mandate

No one gets out without a mandate. I either choose to accept it (and act purposefully to achieve it), or I allow it to die of neglect, a sure path to regret. The Certainty Principle forces me accept that my personal domain of accountability is inescapable.

I must reconcile the one thing that makes me worthy of being a human being. It is worth pretending that accountability to my mandate is eternal due to the certainty and confidence that such commitment delivers. Just as Pascal's Dilemma led the mathematician to the conclusion that he had no choice but full abidance to his faith, TCP leads me to the conclusion that I must abide my mandate. Identity addiction intoxicates me, and like a junkie, identity obscures purpose. To discover the mandate that drives my purpose, I must recognize identity for the game it is. I must stop my brain from wasting its time, focusing instead on doing my duty. Identity is merely a clown costume I have assembled over the years to give my brain meaning. All the while, my true meaning is only solving the problems and completing the tasks in faithful service to the reason I am on the planet. My mandate moves me, otherwise I am dead.

But how do I find it? Stripping away the artificial adornments of identity eventually reveals my reality of purpose. Humility eventually manifests meaning. A mandate that requires an individual to dress as a clown exhibits a persona that appears frivolous, even deprecating to the outside world. But to excel in such work requires an all-in commitment to the important purpose of generating laughter. Failing to discover my mandate only means I will be constantly humiliated until my identity is sufficiently devolved that my brain can finally recognize my mandate.

14.5 — Programming Certainty

The key to programming Certainty is learning how to program the brain. Programming my brain is a two-part process:

- Freeing up memory and bandwidth

- Installing a fresh image of the brain's operating system.

"Image" is a programming term referring to the serialized code of a clean (uncorrupted) version of the operating system. Similarly, in TCP terms, the "TCP Image" is a "fresh" copy of instructions that direct my brain to operate free of the corrupting effects of outcome- and identity-dependence.

But before I can install Certainty, I need to learn how to delete from my brain the residue of synthetic stories and poisoned pictures that consume my capacity to think and act efficiently, effectively, and independently.

My brain will manifest what matters to it, and erase what doesn't matter. My first step is to learn to erase. In brain mechanics, erasing is accomplished by limiting the kind of content my brain is permitting to "clock in." If I consistently deny my brain the time needed to process thoughts unaligned with my mandate, it will soon dismiss such thinking altogether. If I keep "time-starving" my toxic thinking, it will soon pass away.

> *"The best thing you can do for death is ride off from it."*
> McMurtry, 1985

The brain is plastic. It adapts to what is practiced. Learning to starve uncertainty takes time. But the payoff is big: Liberation from detractions and confidence in achieving what is important. Confidence is formed by replacing the dead code with The Certainty Principle affirmation.

Forever My Horizons
Manifest My Mandates
Account My Incomes
Surrender My Outcomes
Depose My Identity

NΩ

CHAPTER 15

THE CERTAINTY PRINCIPLE:
—— LIVING BEFORE THE MAST ——

*"I did not wish to take a cabin passage, but rather to go before
the mast and on the deck of the world,
for there I could best see the moonlight amid the mountains.
I do not wish to go below now."*
THOREAU, WALDEN, 1854

Passivity is the opposite of The Certainty Principle. A passive approach to living always delivers a gray life of sustained mental pain and suffering because inaction is the root cause of most suffering. Thoreau's famous "before the mast" passage challenges passivity. But in the following paragraph he delivers the powerful pay-off:

*"… if one advances
confidently in the
direction of his dreams,
and endeavors to
live the life which
he has imagined,
he will meet with a
success unexpected in
common hours."*

So, what is my pay-off for adopting The Certainty Principle? What is the value of rejecting passivity and learning to comport myself with a demeanor that is calm and confidently optimistic? What is the benefit of an operational perspective of unlimited possibility through action? What is the day-to-day, instant-to-instant benefit of a bias to action as dictated by my natural mandate — unencumbered by delusions of a distinct identity? And is there enough value in such a principle to justify the work that's required to program TCP into the operating system of my decision-making process? Is it even important to have such a guiding principle at all?

With most learning, I take what lessons I can as I encounter them, and make them my own, as dictated by convenience and my comfort level. And I scurry back to the familiar when survival of my identity feels threatened. Same here. Maybe the reader discovers something helpful, a tip or two with quick integration and easy application.

Most learning, with most people, is of this type: Passive. But there is another type of learning, dedicated and deliberate. Competency Learning begins with a plan to change. Man is a verb, not a noun. Passivity makes us animal-like. Our capacity for committing to change is the central quality of being human. Only humans have the choice of change, and that choice distinguishes us. In nature, all change is dictated by evolutionary forces. Only in humans is change dominated by the will to transform ourselves.

Understanding this human dynamic is the key to understanding all important human creations on earth. No pyramids get built, no civilizations rise, no economies grow, and no political systems evolve without the decisions of a few who tenaciously acted on their mandate. The decisions of these few who were so empowered has had an impact on the many.

Their mandates may be virtuous or afflictive. TCP addresses this problem because afflictive mandates are always based on the vanity of the outcome-centered identities. And that is antithetical to TCP. NΩ

Chapter 16
Coda

My Horizon is Forevered. My Mandate is Manifested. My Incomes are Accounted. My Outcomes are Surrendered. My identity is Deposed.

These principles define the instants within which all things manifest in my life. When I wake up in the morning, The Certainty Principle retrieves the direction of my decisions and my next actions, then disciplines my brain's natural randomness. I seldom need someone else directing me, because TCP dictates my priorities. My accountability to TCP exceeds forever, while attachment to the vanity of identity is gone in an instant. My horizon defines my limitations as an individual, so my possibilities are both unlimited and inescapable. My reality is here. I'm elevated to the point of embracing the way things really are, while rejecting any notion that conceit and conditionals have permission to dictate my destiny.

I am no longer a slave to outcomes because my mission is far greater than any particular outcome can influence. Failure and success are subjective imposters, never taken too seriously. It is my action that matters. I will not be defeated by any particular failure. I will not be elevated by any particular success. Failure enables refinement of my methods of action, and success simply disciplines my will to keep things moving. Both are servants of Certainty.

The central focus of my duties always points to my forever horizon. This is the case, regardless of my hopes, fears, sentiments, and regrets. What I hope for, fear, long for, or suffer with is vanity — a concoction my brain builds while seeking to satisfy its persistent organic hunger for deciphering rational meaning.

Reality itself, defies reason, because reality is not a thing confined within the domain of mortal reasoning. Cognition is a reality-modeling device that enables us to create and refine our skill to predict and manifest outcomes through action. But brain work is not reality itself. Neither is it what defines me.

It is futile to ask what the future holds, because with TCP there are only the actions I take now in service to my horizon. The "future," per se, is meaningless. Decisions are meaningful. Likewise, decisions, in and of themselves, are secondary because what matters is my objective — where I am now on the path to that objective, and problem-solving the next action step that is required to get me there.

I can (and do) deliberate on, and make, decisions all day long that fail to execute. TCP demotes making decisions, and promotes taking actions, because when something is important, it is naturally actionable. When it is not important, it is, well ... not important. Lifetimes are wasted by people who fail to recognize this fundamental law. That which demands action is what matters. This can only be understood when there is clarity about what is on the horizon, which can only be accurately seen through a very long-term temporal awareness. Adopting TCP means transforming everything you think you are into your mandate, as described by your "forever horizon."

Remember: All live under the same sky, but not all have the same horizon. Surrendering to the long horizon transforms life, because you become your actions and are no longer a victim of circumstance.

Like Newton's First Law, the force of my core principles will determine the trajectory of my life, and at a rate proportional to my level of commitment to that core. If my principles are important and my commitment is lasting, no obstacle appears insurmountable or at least unavoidable, over the long horizon. This is the heart of individual certainty. There is no objectively right or wrong answer to the question of such a commitment. It is an adventure every human being either decides to accept or abandon to others who are more courageous. I know because I've abandoned it many times. But the hounds of uncertainty are relentless, and the only escape is capitulation to the decisive life.

The dull reader would not have read this far. Most men live lives of quiet desperation because they fear confronting the cause. TCP suggests that desperation is merely the consequence of never having deeply evaluated and adopted the personal principles that naturally qualify one's value in each and every instant.

How do I learn to value myself? Once I know I must, the best starting place I've found is Bogle's Law: My horizon is forever.

If I can muster the courage to confront the primary reality that my individual accountability is absolute and never ending, the rest is easy. There is no universal tonic to uncertainty, because the solution lies in my individual decision to escape the temporal illusion and confront the fact of "forever." I must either discover my individual guiding light of certainty, or revert to the desperation of the herd. This is the great choice, and my choice is The Certainty Principle NΩ

BIBLIOGRAPHY

Achievement, A. A. (1991, February 1). *The First Man To Break the Sound Barrier*. Academy of Achievement. https://www.achievement.org/achiever/general-chuck-yeager/

Adenauer, K. (1972). *Readers Digest*. New York: Readers Digest.

Adler, J. &. (1974). "Decision" making in Bacteria Chemotactic Response. *Science*, 1292-4.

Aurelius, M. (AD c. 170). *Meditations*. Rome.

Beesley, L. (1912). *The Loss of the SS Titanic: Lessons by One of The Survivors*. London: Mariner Books.

Bennett, J. (2019, December 19). *FACTTANK*. Pew Research Center. https://www.pewresearch.org/fact-tank/2019/12/09/veteran-households-in-u-s-are-economically-better-off-than-those-of-non-veterans/

Bezos, J. (2008). *Crazy Billionaires Speak*. Hodderway Books.

Bible, K. J. (1611). *King James Bible*.

Bion, W. (1961). *Experiences In Groups*. Human Relations.

Blake, W. (1793). *The Marriage of Heaven and Hell*. London.

Blau, H. (2015, January 22). *Telomere extension turns back aging clock in cultured human cells*. Blau Lab, Stanford University. http://web.stanford.edu/group/blau/

Bo Xing, Y.-C. L.-J. (2016). *Norepinephrine versus Dopamine, Interaction Modulating Synaptic Function*. Brain Research, 217-233.

Bogle, J. C. (2013, October 4). *The Bogle eBlog*. Malvern, PA, US.

Bogle, J. C. (n.d.). *The Bogle eBlog*. http://johncbogle.com/wordpress/

Boole, G. (1854). *The Laws of Thought*. Cambridge: Cambridge University Press.

Buffett, W. (2018, August 30). CNBC *Interview with Warren Buffett*. (B. Quick, Interviewer)

Burns, R. (1786). Kilmarnock Edition *"To A Mouse"*. Edinburgh: John Wilson.

Burns, R. (1786). *Poems, Chiefly in the Scottish Dialect*. Kilmarnock: John Wilson.

Callahan, S. (2008, July 2008). *The Stonecutters and the Cathedral Builder*. Anecdote. https://www.anecdote.com/2008/07/the-stonecutters-cathedral-builder/

Carnegie, D. (1936). *How to Win Friends and Influence People*. New York: Simon and Schuster.

Cenedella, M. (2016, April 12). *Career Advice*. Ladders. https://www.theladders.com/career-advice/leonardo-da-vincis-resume

Clapton, E., & Gordon, J. (1971). *Layla* [Recorded by E. Clapton]. Miami, Florida, US.

Commission, B. W. (1912, July 30). *British Wreck Commissioner's Inquiry, Day 8*. Titanic Inquiry Project. https://www.titanicinquiry.org/BOTInq/BOTInq08Stewart02.php

Contrera, J. (2016, December 11). *Arts and Entertainment.* Washington Post. https://www.washingtonpost.com/ news/arts-and-entertainment/wp/2016/12/11/bob-dylan-is-sorry-he-didnt-show-up-to-accept-the-nobel-prize/

Covey, S. R. (1989). *The 7 Habits of Highly Effective People.* New York: Free Press.

Crockett, D. (1834). *A Narrative of the Life of David Crockett.* Baltimore: E.L.Carey & A.Hart.

da Vinci, L. (ca. 1520). *Codex Atlanticus.* Milan: Pompeo Leoni.

Darden, L. (1996). Generalizations In Biology. *Studies In History and Philosophy of Science Part A*, pp. 409-419.

Darley , J., & Latane, B. (1968). Bystander Intervention In Emergencies: Diffusion of Responsibility. *Journal of Personality and Social Psychology*, 377-383.

Earhart, A. (1932). *The Fun Of It.* New York: Harcourt, Brace & Co.

Epictetus. (AD c. 125). *The Enchiridion.* Herapolis.

Finkelstein, D. (1958). Past-Future Asymmetry of Gravitational Field of a Point Particle. *Physical Review*, 965.

Frankl, V. (1946). *Man's Search For Meaning.* Vienna: Vertag fur Jugend and Volk.

Franklin, B. (2019, July 3). *A Man Wrapped Up in Himself Makes a Very Small Bundle.* Quote Investigator. https:// quoteinvestigator.com/2019/03/07/bundle/

Gansberg, M. (1964, March 27). 37 Who Saw Murder Didn't Call Police. *New York Times*, p. 1.

Gautama, S. (c. 450 BC). *Buddhavacana*. India.

Gow, P., & Rookwood, J. (2008). Doing it for the Team - Examining the Causes of Hooliganism in English Football. *Journal of Qualitative Research in Sports Studies*, 71-82.

Hagan, M. J., & Sladek, M. R. (2018). Event-related Clinical Distress in College Students: responses to the 2016 U.S. Presidential Election. *Journal of American College Health*.

Heisenberg, W. (1927). Über den anschaulichen Inhalt der quantentheoretischen Kinematik und Mechanik. *Zeitschrift für Physik*, 172-198.

Hertzfeild, A. (1981, February). *Reality Distortion Field*. Folklore. https://www.folklore.org/StoryView. py?story=Reality_Distortion_Field.txt

History Magazine. (1999, October). *The Longbow*. History. http://www.history-magazine.com/longbow.html

Honnald, A. (2019, June 25). *A Soul Freed/Aspen Institute*. (B. Stephens, Interviewer)

Honnold, A. (2020, January 21). *Alex Honnold Goes Undercover on the Internet*. GQ Sports. https://binged.it/3cJIh9Z

Honnold, A. (2015). *Alone On The Wall*. New York: W.W.Norton & Company.

Hoorens, V. (1993). Self-enhancement and Superiority Biases in Social Comparison. *European Review of Social Psychology*, pp. 113-139.

Jobs, S. (2005, June 14). *Bing.com*. https://www.bing.com/videos/search?q=steve+jobs+commencement+address&view=detail&mid=256ECF6D-1209B7AF39EF256ECF6D1209B7AF39EF&FORM=VIRE

Justin, K., & Dunning, D. (1999). Unskilled and Unaware of It: How Difficulties in Recognizing One's Own Incompetence Lead to Inflated Self-Assessments. *Journal of Personality and Social Psychology*, pp. 1121-1134.

Koshland, D., & Sanders, D. (1989). Identification of Phosphorylation of the Chemotaxis Response Regulator Protein. *The Journal of Biological Chemistry*, 21770-8.

Kurzweil, R., & Grossman, MD, T. (2004). *Fantastic Voyage*. Allentown: Rodale.

Lee, H. (1960). *To Kill A Mockingbird*. New York: J.B. Lippincott & Co.

Lemaitre, B. (2016, October). Connecting the Obesity and the Narcissism Epidemics. *Medical Hypothesis*, pp. 10-19.

Liccione, A. (2012, September). *Anthony Liccione*. Anthony Liccione: http://anthony-liccione.wix.com/soi7

Light, D. D. (2019). *The Certainty Principle*. Philadelphia: L & S LTD, Publishers.

Lincoln, A. (1862, January 1). *Annual Message to Congress*. Washington, D.C.

London, J. (1903). *Call of the Wild*. New York: Macmillan.

Lorenz, E. N. (1972, December 29). *Predictability; Does the Flap of a Butterfly's Wings in Brazil Set Off a Tornado in Texas?* www.mit.edu: http://eaps4.mit.edu/research/Lorenz/ Butterfly_1972.pdf

M. Jagger/K. Richards. (1968, November 18). *You Can't Always Get What You Want*. (T. R. Stones, Performer) Olympic Studios, London, UK.

Mackay, C. (1841). *Extraordinary Popular Delusions and the Madness of Crowds*. London: Richard Bentley.

Mallory, G. (1923, March 18). Climbing Mt Everest is the Work for Supermen. *New York Times*.

McMurtry, L. (1985). *Lonesome Dove*. New York: Simon & Schuster.

Melzi, F. (1519, May). *Personal Correspondence*. Amboise, France.

Messner, R. (1971, #15). *The Murder of the Impossible*. Mountain.

Milchman, A., & Rosenberg , A. (1998). *Postmodernism and the Holocaust*. Atlanta: Rodopi.

Mirandola, G. P. (1486). *Oration on the Dignity of Man*. Florence.

Mischel, W., & al., e. (1972). "Cognitive and Attentional Mechanisms In Delay Of Gratification. *Journal of Personality and Social Psychology*, 204-218.

Nash, Jr., J. F. (1950). Equilibrium points in n-person games. *PNAS*, 48-49.

OECD . (2017). *Obesity Update 2017.* Paris: OECD.

Parker, F. (1989, February 15). *Conversation: Dave Light and Fess Parker,* San Francisco.

Parker, T. (1850, May 29). *The American Idea.* (T. Parker, Performer) Anti-Slavery Convention, Boston, MA.

Pascal, B. (1653). *Treatise On Air Pressure.*

Pascal, B. (1670). Pensées. In B. Pascal, *Pensées* (p. #272). Paris: Desfrez.

Pascal, B. (1670). Pensees. *Pascal's Wager.* Paris.

Patton, G. S. (1947). *War As I Knew It.* New York: Houghton Mifflin Harcourt Publishing.

Paul, S. (n.d.). Corinthians 14:8. *The Standard Christian Bible.*

Pearson, K. (1905). *The Problem of the Random Walk.* Nature, 294.

Pigafetta, A. (1525). *Relazione del Prima Viaggio Inforno al Mondo.* Venice.

Plato. (380 BC). *The Republic.* Ancient Greece.

Rousseau, J.-J. (1762). *The Social Contract.* Amsterdam: Marc Michel Rey.

Salu, Y. (2013, June 9). The Role of the Amygdala in the Development of Sexual Arousal. *Journal of Human Sexuality*.

Santayana, G. (1905). *Reason In Common Sense*. New York: Scribner's.

Shakespeare, W. (1600). *Henry V, Part II*. London: Millington and Busby.

Sheff, D. (1985, February). Playboy Interview with Steve Jobs. *Playboy*.

Silverman, S. (2020, January 27). *Leadership Lessons from the Challenger: Face the Brutal Facts of Reality*. BizJournals. com. https://www.bizjournals.com/philadelphia/ news/2020/01/27/leadership-lessons-from-the- challenger-disaster.html

Smythe, F. (1934). *Camp 6*. London.

Sophocles. (429 BC). *Oedipus Rex*. (T. Elders, Performer) Athens.

Su, Q. G. (2019, February 10). *The Chinese Proverb of 'Sai Weng Lost His Horse'*. ThoughtCo. https://www.thoughtco.com/ chinese-proverbs-sai-weng-lost-his-horse-2278437

Tarpey, M. (2014, August 7). *Pressroom*. CareerBuilder. https://www.careerbuilder.com/share/aboutus/pressre- leasesdetail.aspx?sd=8%2F7%2F2014&id=pr837&ed=12% 2F31%2F2014

Thompson, R. F. (1966). Habituation: A Model Phenomenon for the Study of Neural Substrates. *Psychic*. Rev., 16-43.

Thoreau, H. D. (1854). *Walden*. Boston: Ticknor & Fields.

Thoreau, H. D. (1854). *Walden or Life In The Woods*. Boston: Ticknor & Fields.

Trepany, C. (2020, February 6). *Celebrities*. USA Today. https://www.usatoday.com/story/entertainment/celebrities/2020/02/05/kobe-bryant-gayle-king-sparks-outrage-questions-rape-charge/4672566002/

Tribunal, N. (1947, October 23). *Nuremberg Trials Project*. Harvard Law School. https://bit.ly/2RVMcIQ

Turing, A. (1950). Computing Machinery and Intelligence. *Mind, LIX*, 433-460.

Turing, A. (1950). Computing Machinery and Intelligence. *Mind*, pp. 433-60.

Tzu, L. (4th Century B.C.). *Tao Te Ching*. China.

Tzu, L. (4th Century BC). *Tao Te Ching*. Chujen, China.

Tzu, S. (5th Century BC). *The Art of War*. China.

van Dijk, W., van Koningsbruggen, G., & Ouwerkerk, J. (2011, August 30). Self-Esteem, Self-Affirmation and Schadenfreude. Emotion, *American Psychological Association*, pp. 1441-1445.

Wachowski, A., Wachowski, L. (Writers), Wachowski, A., & Wachowski, L. (Directors). (1999). *The Matrix* [Motion Picture].

Williams, D. t. (1993). *Lincoln On Leadership*. New York: Warner Books.

Yangming, W. (1996). The Philosophy of Wang Yangming. In D. S. Nivison, *The Ways of Confucianism* (pp. 217-231). Chicago: Open Court Press.

NΩ